# Prais
# Sigi Osag

★★★★★ "This is the book I have been searching for … Great book … full of practical advice. This one is a page-turner!"

**Christiaan Murphy, Amazon Customer**

"Here is a book that most certainly gets some key messages across … If you're involved with stakeholders then it's most definitely worth a read, and I bet you recognize yourself somewhere in there."

**David Abbott, Vice President & General Manager, Terex AWP, China**

"Sigi coached our team to improve our effectiveness and functional competence … he helped me sharpen my own professional capabilities … a brilliant coach and mentor."

**Ben Wilmot, Programme Manager, Ericsson**

"His content is powerful, concise and invaluable … will have a long-lasting, immensely positive effect upon the Burberry team."

**Stuart Pemble, Group CPO, Burberry**

# Sweet Stakeholder Love

POWERFUL INSIGHTS AND TACTICS

TO DEAL WITH STAKEHOLDER ISSUES BETTER AND

ACHIEVE MORE SUCCESS AT WORK

SIGI OSAGIE

First published in 2021 by EPG Solutions Limited
Registered Office: The Old Bakery, Blackborough Road, Reigate, Surrey RH2 7BU, United Kingdom
www.sigiosagie.com

Contains extracts from earlier works by Sigi Osagie © 2006–2021

Editing by Karen Morton Editorial Services
Cover design by Tanja Prokop
Interior design, formatting and typesetting by Graciela Aničić
www.bookcoverworld.com

ISBN (paperback): 978-1-8384892-0-5
ISBN (e-book): 978-1-8384892-1-2

To Love.

Thank you for the magic.

# CONTENTS

# AUTHOR'S NOTE

Everybody has issues with "stakeholders".

Perhaps the only exception is the mad scientist locked away in his laboratory, working in isolation on experiments to discover the next breakthrough in time travel or how to tame the sun and the moon.

But even he will eventually have to deal with some stakeholders when he comes to commercialise his invention.

Even almighty CEOs, who seem all-dominant and supremely in command without having to pander to anyone else, have issues with varied stakeholders inside and outside the organisation – for starters, their board colleagues, the investors or owners of the business and, quite likely, the bank. They must be savvy with these stakeholders to remain in the job for any length of time.

Hard-charging professionals are frequently astounded by the massive improvements in their effectiveness and work success that come from savvy stakeholder management. I was too.

I got my first executive job, as a global director in a FTSE 250 multinational, some years after arriving in the UK as a near barefoot and penniless immigrant. It was a fourteen-year adventure filled with lots of struggle, hard slog and learning. One of the most crucial things I learned on that journey was the importance of cultivating sound stakeholder relationships. Whether I was setting up a new function somewhere in Europe or driving a change programme in Asia or America, engaging people shrewdly and winning them over to my work agenda has always been a critical requirement for my success.

Your own success at work is just as much tied to your stakeholder relationships. As is your overall well-being; because most of us are spending more and more time at work than with our families and loved ones. When we have turbulent stakeholder relationships at work, with the inherent and sometimes unspoken conflicts they bring, the resulting tensions and negative emotions often carry over into our private lives and affect us adversely – sometimes in ways we may not see.

Conversely, the positive vibes that come from healthy stakeholder relationships help us enjoy work much more and they ooze into our life outside work. Then things just feel great. It makes life easier and sweeter. Hitting that sweet spot is essential for our work performance and gaining fulfilment from the work itself.

We often mean different things when we talk about "stakeholders". Sometimes we're referring to the various colleagues or co-workers we interact with at work, which may include our direct bosses and immediate team members. Other times we're referring specifically to people who impact and are impacted by the work we do. Either way, maintaining positive relationships with these folks is a vital element of finding our groove and orchestrating brilliant success at work. And what you'll learn from this book will help you immensely in that regard.

You will gain powerful insights and approaches to help you up your game and become more savvy with managing your stakeholders.

Since we spend so much of our lifetimes at work, our experiences with stakeholders typically form key aspects of our life stories. The experiences themselves are stories, whether they're good ones or bad ones. And stories are central to our existence as human beings. We're creating stories of all sorts all the time – stories of ourselves as parents, spouses, lovers, daughters, sons, friends, and as professionals in the workplace.

We're continuously writing and telling our individual stories by our thoughts, feelings and actions, including our interactions with stakeholders. And the stories we tell ourselves, consciously or unconsciously, shape our lives.

We're all storytellers; it's how we make sense of the world around us. Psychological studies and brain-mind research show that telling, reading or listening to stories is one of the most compelling and impactful ways to stimulate our brains. It arouses our senses in ways that amplify our perception and learning tremendously. That's why I chose to share what I've learned through this story, which is based on true events.

It's a story of frustration, angst and despondence, the negative emotions that blighted my work life and hampered my progress.

Yet it's also a tale of triumph, of remarkable learn-ing and growth that evolved from several stakeholder challenges, probably similar to the stakeholder issues you face today.

Quite often, when faced with such challenges it's easy to fall prey to feelings of vulnerability. But you're never truly powerless in such situations – there's so much you can do to change things and create productive stakeholder relationships for yourself.

This book is packed with practical ideas, guidance and tactics to help you deal with your stakeholders more effectively. It will engage, inform and inspire you to boost your stakeholder management skills, and thus gain greater success and fulfilment at work.

It's not a textbook or academic treatise filled with technical mumbo-jumbo, copious research findings or theoretical concepts. It's a book based on real-life experiences with stakeholders in the workplace, underpinned by proven principles and techniques – approaches which you yourself can apply to hit that sweet spot with your stakeholders at work.

# LEARNING FROM A
# MASTER

# CHAPTER 1

I SAT AT MY DESK fuming. I can well imagine that my colleagues in the open-plan office could actually see the steam coming out of my ears. I was clearly too incensed to concentrate on the task I was meant to be working on; that was even more galling – the task, or what led up to it, was the very source of my anger and frustration.

I gave up on the task in the end and picked up the phone instead. I rang Ralph's secretary and asked to see him, telling her it was urgent and important.

She said she'd let him know and call me back with a time for the appointment I wanted.

I continued to stew in my emotions while awaiting the call-back. It didn't help that my mind kept replaying the events of that morning which had created my predicament. In my mind's eye, I was fully justified in being angry and frustrated with Ralph. How could he have done that!

When I'd joined C-MEG Corporation a year or so earlier, I had been over the moon. While coming to the tail end of my part-time MBA studies, I had devoted a significant amount of time and effort to thinking through and deciding my career direction. I saw the MBA as a launch pad that I could leverage to move my career in any number of directions. And I wanted to get it right. I even invested some serious moolah in the services of a career coach.

The job with C-MEG was exactly what I had decided I wanted to do next: an internal business consultancy role in a blue-chip multinational company. You couldn't get more blue-chip than C-MEG Corporation, a multibillion-pound behemoth of a conglomerate with interests in several sectors and tentacles stretching to all corners of the globe.

I was lucky in some senses (then again, they do say luck is opportunity meeting preparation) – C-MEG had decided to set up an internal business consultancy unit, running process improvement projects and large-scale organisational change programmes, at about the same time I was going through my career deliberations. My timing couldn't have been more fortuitous, as if the gods were smiling down on me.

But there was nothing fortuitous or divine about my meeting earlier that morning. Exasperation was all that came of it.

As often happens with many large corporate businesses, C-MEG had recently been through yet another reorganisation. This time it was massive. The whole group had been completely restructured into three global divisions. For a corporation with about 100,000 employees worldwide, the ramifications of the ensuing restructuring were like seismic shifts that shook the entire global organisation. And Ralph Patrick was bang in the centre of one of those ramifications.

Ralph had been appointed as Executive Vice President (EVP) of Global Procurement and Supply Chain Management (PSCM) for the newly formed Electromechanical Division. But he was an emperor with no empire. The thirteen or so businesses brought together to form the "Electromech" division were as disparate as they come, each with its own distinct PSCM operations and organisation. Ralph knew he had to fix it.

I was the fix-it guy. As Ralph's assigned internal business consultant, I led the transformation project to integrate and harmonise these disjointed PSCM operations into one consolidated divisional infrastructure.

Well, as anyone who has led large change programmes will tell you, where there's change, there's usually pain. And when it's in a big business, the pain can sometimes be so senseless and frustrating as to make you feel like jumping out of a tenth-floor window and slitting your throat on the way down. As I would come to discover.

I had been running the Electromech Global PSCM project for a while and was enjoying it immensely. I had brought on board the structured change management disciplines we used on all our business improvement projects, and it was proving truly beneficial.

Ralph had agreed with me that the project Steering Group must include three other EVPs whose functional areas would be significantly impacted by the change. These people were my most important stakeholders, second only to Ralph himself, who I saw as my prime stakeholder. Richard Tilman, Giuseppe "Peppe" Mancini and Matthew Gresham all seemed very likeable. We all got together fortnightly at our prescheduled Steering Group meetings, where I updated them on the project progress and got their feedback and guidance.

In the ego-filled world of large corporate organisations, working with EVPs, or reporting to one, is like working with God's own lieutenants. These guys are often just a step or two below the main board on the greasy pole we call an organisational structure. Most mere mortals can't even get to speak to these demigods on the phone, never mind have face-to-face meetings with them. And here was yours truly mixing with them regularly. I thought I was going up in the world. Until that fateful meeting when my bubble was burst.

Ralph and the other three EVPs had proved extremely valuable, both collectively and as individuals. Each one of them had brought something worthwhile to the project. And together they had done exactly what a steering group should do: steered the project and helped me clear major obstacles whenever progress was hindered.

I liked the dynamics between us all – they often joked with me or teased me about something or other, and the camaraderie amongst the four of them seemed great.

That lovely chemistry aided us in reaching agreement on several issues. One of those was my insistence up front that they refrain from telling me what to do; rather, they must let me get on with the job but challenge my approach whenever necessary to ensure robustness. For instance, rather than trying to tell me how the integrated PSCM infrastructure and operating model should be configured, they must let me carry out a full, rigorous analysis and assessment to reach the optimal recommended solution.

I had indeed gone through a very detailed analysis of the existing situation in all aspects of PSCM across the new division. With the help of my small team of business analysts, I had fully mapped out various operational processes, how strategic decisions were made, the functional teams in each business unit, the IT systems in use, etc. I had even used some external benchmarking to sanity-check our efforts, in addition to having numerous discussions with many stakeholders in different geographies and functional areas to understand their needs and priorities.

It was a laborious and painstaking exercise, not made any easier by recurrent attempts of a few stakeholders to distort the picture of the existing situation and thus influence my judgement.

It was all quite mind-boggling.

But then again, creating an integrated PSCM function for a two-billion-pound global division was never going to be a walk in the park.

I had presented my "As-is" findings at a previous Steering Group meeting several weeks ago. Today's meeting, earlier this morning, was when I presented my recommendations on the "To-be" model. All through the project I made sure I stayed aligned to Ralph – as the Project Sponsor I wanted him to always be fully up to speed with important issues. One of those was my recommendations for the integrated structure.

A few days before the Steering Group meeting I talked Ralph through my recommendations. I knew that the resulting carve-outs of several functional areas, related job changes and possible redundancies across the division would be a hard sell for the folks impacted, and possibly some divisional executives. So I wanted to ensure my Project Sponsor was also my number-one cheerleader.

Ralph had agreed with my thinking and approach, and he sanctioned the recommended organisational structure and business case. So when I walked into the Steering Group meeting that morning, the last person I expected to oppose my recommendations was Ralph.

# CHAPTER 2

IN HINDSIGHT, WITH SEVERAL YEARS' experience as a senior executive and change leader now behind me, I can see that I was quite naïve. I hadn't yet fully grasped the intricate and sometimes bewildering ways large organisations function.

You'd think that as someone who had completed an MBA not that far back I would have been well versed in such matters. It's probably not an unreasonable expectation; I had even done a module on my MBA course titled "Understanding Organisations". But academic learning in a faculty of business studies at any university can be very different from experiential learning in the Faculty of Hard Knocks at the University of Life.

Walking into that meeting with the expectation of "Steering Group Approval" as a foregone conclusion shows how inexperienced I was at such matters.

I knew PSCM like the back of my hand. I'd always prided myself on proactively managing my career to give me exposure to all functions across the end-to-end supply chain management spectrum; in fact, that was why I had been assigned to Ralph as his project lead. But my subsequent experience has shown me that success at work is less about technical knowledge than it is about mastering the "soft" issues, like interpersonal relationships, organisational dynamics, engaging and winning stakeholders over, and so on.

My ordeal in that Steering Group meeting proved it.

Despite my best attempts and approaching my "sell" from several different angles, I was unable to win over two of the EVPs. Peppe and Richard were both strongly opposed to my recommended structure for the integrated PSCM organisation. Matthew seemed rather unperturbed; he had enthusiastically agreed with my recommendations when I had outlined them moments before, but now didn't respond to Peppe's and Richard's opposition – he didn't try to disagree with them or argue for my proposal. But the person who stole the show was Ralph. Unlike Matthew, he didn't just sit there seemingly neutral but actively agreed with Peppe and Richard.

*Sacré bleu!* Ralph had blindsided me!

How could he? Why was he doing this? What was he up to? …

These thoughts raced through my mind as I sat there dumbfounded, my brain refusing to take in what my eyes and ears were perceiving.

Ralph and I had gone through this very same presentation only a few days ago. He had asked one or two questions, which I'd addressed to his satisfaction. And he had emphatically confirmed at the end of our meeting that as the Project Sponsor he endorsed my recommendations. And now, here he was agreeing with Richard and Peppe that my recommended structure wasn't appropriate.

To say I was baffled would be the understatement of the century. I was even more incensed by the bizarre alternative structure Richard and Peppe wanted: a divisional PSCM organisational structure with two heads.

I'm sure I failed in masking my exasperation as I asked how any organisation could function effectively with two chiefs. I tried to argue rationally that the resulting PSCM organisation was bound to end up being dysfunctional, as having two people at the top was the first sign of organisational ineffectiveness. But my arguments fell on deaf ears, including Ralph, who continued to agree with Peppe and Richard, much to my annoyance.

It was that annoyance and frustration that was chewing me up as I sat at my desk waiting for Ralph's secretary to ring me back.

I had left the Steering Group meeting grudgingly agreeing to change the proposed PSCM structure to what Peppe and Richard wanted, before it would be ratified by the Steering Group and thence the divisional board. But I knew it was complete rubbish – you can't have two captains of a ship and expect the organisation to operate smoothly and satisfactorily. It was idiotic. And I didn't want to be part of it; I didn't want my name associated with the project that created what I knew would be a doomed organisational change.

At that point in my career, I was aware that some managers can sometimes be befuddled or incapacitated by events or a change of circumstances around them, especially when it involves significant decisions they must make. They become hesitant, indecisive or paralysed outright into inaction, like a rabbit caught in the headlights.

They might try to disguise their dithering and ineptitude by shifting the focus to something else, like the bureaucracy of the decision-making process, asking for more and more information or fussing over meaningless trivia. I was aware of the need to help such managers make the right decisions as stakeholders.

But that wasn't the case this time.

In this situation it felt as if *I* was the one being "helped" down a predetermined decision path, a path paved with the foreboding of a grim fate, like being forced to drink from a poisoned chalice.

I was peeved at finding myself in a situation where I had been manoeuvred to agree to do something I strongly disagreed with, something I knew without a shadow of doubt was just wrong. I felt it so intensely it was as if every aspect of my moral compass was screaming, "This is wrong!" Yet I couldn't figure out why these supposedly experienced managers wanted to go down this road. They certainly hadn't justified their preference in any way that made sense. And trying to reason with them had been like trying to have a sensible discussion with lunatics in an asylum.

I felt manipulated. And I guess somewhere in the mishmash of emotions now buffeting me was a huge degree of self-annoyance that, during the discussion, I didn't have the dexterity to handle the three demigods without making myself seem quarrelsome or hostile – especially to stakeholders who were supposed to be on my side. I had felt like an amateur playing against a trio of Olympic gold medallists. And, of course, I'd been absolutely and totally outplayed.

But worst of all, one of those medallists was Ralph.

I was so vexed with him for what felt like a betrayal, more so because I couldn't understand why. I soon would, as my desk phone rang and I heard the man himself say, "Hi Sigi, it's Ralph."

That phone call turned out to be one of the key moments of my career journey.

\*

Ralph said he'd got my message and asked why I wanted to see him. I told him it was to do with the Steering Group meeting earlier that day, and that I felt we were at odds; it didn't make sense for the Project Leader and the Project Sponsor to be in conflict, so it was imperative we discussed things urgently.

I suspect that he sensed my feelings. He told me to meet him, "Downstairs in the car park in ten minutes."

I put the phone down, wondering why he wanted to meet me in the car park, of all places.

"Sigi, do you smoke?" were his words of greeting when I met him downstairs.

He invited me to join him for a drive and I agreed, even though I had no idea where to or why. My thoughts were soon interrupted by the wondrous feeling of luxury as I sank into the plush passenger seat of his Maserati Quattroporte. It was a magnificent-looking car that oozed opulence inside and out, and its conspicuous aesthetic aroused a tinge of envy in me. I remember thinking to myself as I looked around and took in the sumptuous interior: "Wow, is this how the big boys roll? I'd love to have a ride like this when I get to the top."

Ralph drove to a small shopping centre a few miles from C-MEG's campus base and parked in one of the vacant parking spaces. He reached across to the glove compartment, brought out a box of Romeo y Julieta cigars and lit one for himself while offering me another.

I accepted it with thanks. But I was soon almost re-gretting it as I spluttered with coughs after my first puff.

I had never smoked a cigar before. I learned to savour one over the next hour or so as Ralph and I sat talking in his car. He listened quietly to my complaints about his "betrayal" and the stupidity of the suggested alternative PSCM structure. He let me vent completely without interrupting.

Afterwards, when he spoke he did so candidly. He started out by telling me that he liked me. (We hadn't known each other until I turned up at his office for our first meeting as his internal business consultant.) He said he liked the way I had run the project and was impressed with my general professionalism in everything he'd seen and heard of me. He went on to point out a number of positive traits he saw in me, recalling some real-life examples of my behaviour to illustrate his points.

It was all music to my ears, of course.

He asked me about my career ambitions, which I was happy to share with him, though my mind still couldn't quite fathom what all this had to do with the reason we were there. He then told me that if I wanted to climb to the top in my career I would have to learn how to deal with organisational politics. He said that politics and all sorts of skulduggery were often intrinsic elements of the type of large-scale organisational restructuring C-MEG Corporation was going through.

"The higher up you climb, the more you're likely to face these sorts of issues," he continued. "You'll find that some senior executives are occasionally driven by individual agendas and self-interests, not necessarily what's best for the organisation. It's more common than you might think, especially in big companies."

He explained that as a senior executive himself, it was important for him to manage his peer-group relationships while navigating through this political landscape and delivering his business results. To do that successfully, earlier in his career he'd had to learn to orchestrate his moves deftly without burning bridges.

He said I needed to hone my ability to do the same; that developing my navigational prowess as such would be instrumental to my success, especially when operating at senior levels.

I instinctively understood what Ralph meant. Even then, way before I had risen to the ranks of demigods, I always tried to avoid making enemies amongst work colleagues, falling out with stakeholders or being on bad terms with them. Aside from the fact that it's unhealthy for the soul, you just never know what the future holds and if you'll cross paths with them again. Yet avoiding burned bridges of one's own creation and still achieving one's work objectives isn't always plain sailing.

Ralph himself agreed.

"But you'll only become an accomplished sailor by growing your familiarity with the seas and constantly refining your seamanship," he continued. The enigmatic smile on his face and his avuncular tone of voice made him seem like an old sea dog who had sailed through many storms. I imagined this organisational restructuring was just another one.

He moved on to talk about the other key characters pertinent to the PSCM project, particularly the Steering Group members. He explained what the *real* organisational structure in the division was, not the one on the organisational chart; the relationship dynamics and political intrigues involved in the change we were creating; and went on to clarify why Peppe and Richard had opposed my proposal – what they were really up to – and why he himself had adopted the stance he took in the Steering Group meeting that morning.

Apparently, it was all part of a dance. And I didn't even realise I was on the dance floor.

It was my first introduction to truly understanding the art of organisational politics and leveraging interpersonal dynamics. And I was learning from a true master.

As I would come to know later, Ralph had been at the top of the greasy pole for many years in several large companies, and had held senior leadership responsibilities across numerous countries around the globe. He remained not just a survivor but a true big beast. He certainly knew a thing or two.

# CHAPTER 3

THROUGH RALPH'S SKILFUL GUIDANCE I became more adept at reading the organisational landscape and deciphering the machinations that frequently define the conduct of senior-level stakeholders.

Dealing with the myriad of manoeuvres and seemingly irrational behaviours amongst some senior managers often felt like swimming through shark-infested waters. It was one of the most stretching career growth experiences I've been through. There was brown-nosing, narcissism and chicanery aplenty, on top of the customary cover-your-back moves that are sometimes standard operating procedure for some individuals. A psychologist would have had a field day analysing it all. I had many perplexing days, for sure. There were many times I found myself wondering: "Why do I have to waste so much effort on this stuff that's got nothing to do with the real business issues?"

But that's a bit like asking why the sun shines, why the moon glows or why the rooster crows. Or pondering why there's so much poverty in a world with so many riches.

Ralph was right. My subsequent career experience corroborates the lowdown he gave me. Politics, self-interests, hidden agendas and overinflated egos are often part of the executive terrain in many organisations. And learning to steer your way through "this stuff", while nurturing interpersonal relationships and retaining focus on your work goals, is a fundamental requirement to manage senior-level stakeholders successfully. It's really more of an *investment* than a "waste", an investment in your work success.

Interestingly, my own investment yielded an additional return: learning to swim with the sharks without getting eaten forced me to become more aware of my "blind" behaviours – those mannerisms and traits we all have but are unaware of, though they are apparent to others. Our blindness thus inhibits us from appreciating how these behaviours impact on people we interact with.

It can be so easy to become too focused on, or critical about, others' behaviours and forget that our own behaviours are key ingredients for successful stakeholder engagement. Research has revealed that we all have a matrix of behaviours – a mix of what is known and unknown, to us and to others. Understanding your own mix of behaviours is a key part of increasing your self-awareness. And self-awareness is one of the cornerstones of improving individual capability and performance, including our ability to manage relationships with others successfully.

This enhanced self-awareness couldn't have been more timely for me.

At that stage of my career, I was an ambitious Young Turk who didn't suffer fools gladly. I was prone to wear my heart on my sleeve and let my impatience get the better of me from time to time. Inevitably, I unwittingly fell into the trap of occasionally displaying behavioural tendencies which hindered my own effectiveness. This isn't the most productive route to workplace success. And it's definitely not advisable in shark-infested waters.

Shark experts stay alive in the water because they understand shark behaviour and continually expand their understanding. They imbibe the wisdom of St. Francis of Assisi, which Stephen R. Covey reminded us of more recently: "Seek first to understand, then to be understood."

Understanding the behaviours of senior-level stakeholders – some of whom are the biggest and baddest sharks – makes it less taxing to manage relationships with them. If you're clueless about a shark's behaviour or habits, you'll also be clueless about its next move; a chunk of your flesh could be in its jaws before you know it.

The fear of a possible shark bite didn't dampen my ambition. But it brought into sharp focus the requirement to expand my capabilities if I was to survive and thrive in shark-infested waters. I *really* had to learn how to handle senior players adroitly.

And I did. Sometimes, much to my dismay.

I learned so much more about workplace success than anything I'd known before, stuff that you'll find beneficial in your own dealings with sharks and other stakeholders.

For instance, I learned that the formal organisational chart – the one shown to you at your induction or plastered on the corporate intranet – may only ever tell you a little of how things are really "organised", so basing your stakeholder management approach on it may not always yield progress.

The real organisational structure, often created and controlled by the sharks and other big fish, is an informal web of motives and relationships that dictates how things really progress, or don't. It's an ecosystem that can be rife with so many unspoken forces and minefields. For example, Shark A and Shark B who are sworn enemies, or may head competing fiefdoms, and consequently are always on the lookout to profit from opportunities for power grabs; Big Fish X who is a sponsor and protector of Stakeholder Z, and will thus block anything that threatens the position or advancement of her protégé; Stakeholders A, B and C who are entangled in a *ménage à trois* that is as gripping and addictive as nothing you can imagine, and is so all-consuming as to blot out any modicum of common sense they may have had before their sexual entanglement; Big Fish D and Shark C who are tight buddies outside work, play soccer together and will always guard each other's interests come rain or shine; Stakeholder X who has the hots for Stakeholder Y, and as a result will go along with anything Stakeholder Y supports no matter how stupid it is; or Big Fish C who is a virtuoso at stealing credit for other people's work, and will always seek avenues to practise his dirty craft in order to further his status in the organisation – he's probably

seen you and your work on the horizon as another avenue, well before you even identified him as a stakeholder.

If you think these sorts of forces and other similar
dynamics aren't at play in your own organisation to some
degree, you may be grossly mistaken.

The real organisational structure is an important
factor that strongly influences how sharks and other
stakeholders respond to you and your work agenda.

And within that structure, more often than not, some
of the most fruitful nodes of influence that can be easily
neglected are the gatekeepers: the secretaries, personal
assistants and executive assistants who act as aides, guard-
ians and protectors. They usually have more sway in the
ecosystem than many people realise, particularly because
of their roles working so intimately with the sharks and
other big fish. They tend to be in the know, and can
frequently affect the perceptions and perspectives of their
protectee.

Keeping the gatekeeper sweet, and perhaps even
asking for their help or advice outright, can often reap
lucrative rewards.

I also learned the importance of cultivating a depend-
able network of loyal colleagues and allies, and the value

of developing a coalition of support for one's work agenda, especially in the upper echelons of the organisation.

And I learned how one can often generate so many unforeseen positive outcomes by being helpful to others – but this doesn't mean you should become a doormat or a martyr; as the saying goes, you can't set yourself on fire to keep other people warm.

You shouldn't be helpful just because you want something back in return. There's an element of decency about this, something that can easily be forgotten: to treat others as you would like to be treated – keeping in mind that not everyone necessarily wants to be treated in exactly the same way as you do. Yet you should also be aware that the unspoken rule of reciprocity makes it more likely that you will get something back in return, even if that something is simply a more cooperative attitude or more supportive behaviour. It's somewhat like reaping the fruits of the goodwill that you sow, or what some might refer to as karma.

I learned, too, that flexibility is strength. Being able to fluidly adapt your approach helps you deal with a broader range of circumstances and individual characters; a bit like the flexible trees that are more able to withstand the storms because they can bend and sway with the wind.

It's almost a sure thing that you *will* need to bend and sway with the various sorts of stakeholders you'll come across at different points in your career. Some of them will be Supporters, who "get it" and don't need much persuasion or tender loving care, thus demanding relatively less of your energy. But some Supporters can sometimes be over-supportive. They may be so eager in their support that they'll want to run at a hundred miles per hour – possibly in the wrong direction – when you prefer to move at a less frenetic pace. Hence, you may need to shepherd their enthusiasm so they work in synchrony with you, your agenda and the way you roll, rather than zoom off at a tangent.

Other stakeholders might be Crowd-pleasers, who'll say all the right things and act like they're "with you" in meetings and in front of senior managers or key people, but then they'll go off and do something contrary to your requirements or agenda. Dealing with Crowd-pleasers can play havoc with your thoughts and emotions, and you may find yourself teetering between hope and despair over and over again. You may be able to convert some Crowd-pleasers into Supporters through concerted relationship-building and timely and meaningful deeds or results, especially if you *really* make the effort to get in bed with them.

Crowd-pleasers can be exasperating and energy-draining. But probably less so than the final type of stakeholders: the Detractors. If you don't have voodoo magic powers, then you may find yourself wishing for a whole nuclear power station to supply the energy you need to handle your Detractors. Because one Detractor typically requires more energy than it takes to handle a thousand prima donnas. Detractors will always try to fight against your agenda or attack you or your work. They need the greatest relationship-building efforts, requiring lots of nous, staying power, fortitude, self-belief, patience and that flexibility.

But you have to accept and expect that some Detractors may never be won over. Don't let that derail your efforts; just remind yourself that you can't win 'em all, and that's okay, but it shouldn't stop you from trying.

*

It was my efforts at "trying" with the numerous Detractors, Crowd-pleasers and Supporters on the Electromech PSCM project that taught me a number of salient lessons about effective stakeholder management.

For example, that it's usually more effective to step back and think through what's likely to be a more appropriate response or behaviour on your part, before taking action in a specific situation; that applying some give and take may be part of the dance to achieve optimal outcomes, so seeking compromise or finding common ground can sometimes be more advantageous than sticking rigidly to your position when there are disagreements; and that quite often, in conversations with senior-level stakeholders, there's more behind what they say or what they ask, so it's useful to consider what lies behind their words.

Words are tremendously powerful, whether they are expressed in the mind, spoken with the tongue, written with the pen or typed with a keyboard. Words carry energy that can bring joy or misery, can evoke laughter or tears, can lift people up or tear them down. Sweet words of love by lyricists and crooners like Barry White have led to the creation of many new little humans all over the world. And poisonous words of hate by tyrants and evil zealots have led to the destruction of millions of human lives through the ages. Because words transmit impact.

So it's crucial to watch your choice of words in stakeholder conversations. Try to communicate in plain language using terms your stakeholders will comprehend, rather than boring or irritating them with jargon – avoid using gobbledygook they might not understand or buzzwords that'll make their eyes glaze over.

And it's just as important to notice stakeholders' choice and use of words.

Some people use lots of words without really saying anything meaningful. Sometimes, it's because they like the sound of their own voice, or they want to look good in front of others, or they want to show they're smarter than you, or they have nothing concrete to say but would rather not show it. Sometimes people are just nervous, tired, suffering the residual effects of alcohol or too much caffeine, or they may simply be over-talkative by nature and unable to curb their verbal diarrhoea.

Some folks use the act of talking to form their thoughts, shape their opinions or gain clarity on their views. Hence, they're quite likely to appreciate the time and space to get their words out in the way they want to.

Some use their words for personal attacks, and you can become ensnared in the drama that follows if you lose your composure or react with anger, perhaps by counter-attacking them or becoming defensive or argumentative, which often exacerbates the situation and sidetracks you from your core purpose.

Others will use few or no words, keeping their thoughts and opinions to themselves, despite your efforts to engage them. They may be taciturn by nature. Or they may be the sort of political animal who's just watching, not wanting to take sides or show their hand; it could be because they're waiting to see which wind prevails and how the wind blows, then they'll jump on the bandwagon and be more forthcoming with their words.

And some stakeholders use specific words in very deliberate ways to help or to hinder. For example, to bring knowledge or simplicity as a positive contribution, or to create confusion or obfuscation for their own underhand reasons – reasons which may include intentionally concealing their unhelpful behaviours by weaving a camouflage with their words.

Trying to decode people's words requires sincere listening, giving them your full attention as if they're the centre of your world. It also requires listening with your ears, your heart, as well as your behaviour – for example, by maintaining good eye contact without being awkward, and using gestures, like a nod, or phrases like "Okay", "I get you" or "I agree" to reinforce what they're communicating. Voicing your agreement with specific statements a stakeholder makes, even if you disagree with their overall stance or opinion, can sometimes convey solid reassurance that you indeed comprehend what's being relayed to you.

Listening candidly can be a great doorway to reading people better and sensing their true sentiments. We often forget that communication is a two-way street, and each of us has one mouth and two ears – maybe there's a reason for that ratio; perhaps the ratio signifies that we should speak half as much as we listen. An added payback is that a stakeholder who feels that they've been listened to will very likely give you good airtime for your own pitch. Whereas a stakeholder who feels otherwise is unlikely to be attentive to your gist. And there's no point telling your story if your audience isn't tuned in.

Probably more significant than anything else I learned was the importance of always being honest and impeccable, and maintaining one's personal standards and professional ethics.

Your own ethics will be the moral compass that will guide you as you navigate your way through your stakeholder landscape, especially the executive terrain. And you'll need that compass, because you'll probably face some situations that'll test your integrity and trustworthiness. That probability is an inherent facet of developing senior-level stakeholder relationships.

The ability to nurture positive relationships with senior-level stakeholders not only impacts our immediate workplace activities, it can also influence our long-term career development. Many senior-level stakeholders are decent people who want you to succeed and will put the wind in your sails. But you've got to know how to engage them with savvy.

Learning all of this stuff was a pivotal stepping stone on my career path. I couldn't have recognised and taken advantage of this opportunity without Ralph's support. His one-on-one guidance proved a godsend, not just on the remainder of the Electromech PSCM project but many years later too. I grew to respect his insights and counsel, especially as my own leadership career advanced at senior levels.

As I mentioned in one of my articles on talent and success, I learned a lot from my undergraduate and postgraduate degrees and the leadership development programmes I went through at two employers, but I've learned a heck of a lot more about career success from my mentors. And when it comes to organisational re-lationships at senior levels, Ralph was the mentor from whom I learned the most – a fabulous mentor in every sense. He aided my leadership development in so many ways. Meeting him turned out to be one of the greatest blessings of my career journey, a blessing that evolved from what initially seemed like a stakeholder conflict.

# THE MOST DIFFICULT
# STAKEHOLDER

# CHAPTER 4

IT'S INTERESTING THAT RALPH AND I only really got to know each other stemming from the conflict of views in that fateful Steering Group meeting. Life is like that sometimes; it throws us blessings we don't often recognise as such. Or it chooses to package opportunities in "wrapping paper" that makes them look like challenges.

These days, when I sit with project sponsors and senior managers in client organisations before starting an improvement initiative, I typically ask if there are any political factors or organisational dynamics I need to be aware of. And quite often, they are hesitant to tell it as it is. Yet these factors are the things that frequently create barriers, frustrate employees and cause many work initiatives to go awry.

So I frequently find myself elaborating on the importance of laying out these issues up front to give the improvement programme a greater chance of success.

As uncomfortable as it may make some managers and project sponsors feel, I deliberately choose to ask this question because I've come to learn that it's often better to ask stakeholders questions directly rather than make assumptions on anything. And the better the quality of your questions, the more likely you are to derive useful nuggets from the responses you get.

In addition to being straightforward nowadays, I try to maintain my long-held habit of being accessible to colleagues and stakeholders at all levels – including the cleaning lady, the receptionist and the security guard.

Sometimes, some of us can be deliberately distant or even arrogantly aloof with work colleagues and stakeholders. Or we act and speak in ways that inspire fear and insecurity in others. As if we ourselves fear that "familiarity breeds contempt". Or perhaps we espouse those attitudes because we're driven – in a blinkered way – by the principle that "I'm at work to work, not to be anyone's friend". Or maybe we believe that projecting a tough front to everyone at all times is good for our personal brand, and more advantageous than being seen or perceived as open, sympathetic and considerate.

Of course, we are at work to work, although some have found love and long-term close friendships at work. And it's true that some colleagues or stakeholders may take liberties or try to take advantage of us when we're too friendly with them – if we allow it. So, yes, sometimes we may need to be matter-of-fact with some people. But you don't have to be an ogre. Being resolute and being amiable aren't mutually exclusive.

This doesn't mean you need to become bosom buddies with anyone or everyone at work. In fact, there are some risks with workplace friendships, so it's important to establish your ground rules and boundaries that enable you to balance privacy, amity, professional conduct and getting on with what you're paid for.

Yet, all the while, you should remember that amicability and positive workplace relationships bring many benefits related to our happiness and job satisfaction, with research studies showing that this extends to our productivity and quality of work.

At any rate, it's unlikely you'll be able to do anything of high quality with your stakeholders without productive relationships.

Many of those inclinations for aloofness or toughness stem from our ego-centred selves, and often reflect the rational and myopic thinking of our minds. But our hearts have skin in the game too. And our hearts know us better than we know ourselves. So just as it's fruitful to listen with your heart, it's also gainful to "think" with your heart – even if only every now and then. When you do, you'll find that, rather than being cold or intimidating with stakeholders, it's usually more beneficial to make people feel relaxed about talking to you.

As well as giving my heart the baton as often as necessary, I also make a supreme effort to drop my "mask" – the persona we often adopt in the workplace – or not wear one at all, so that stakeholders can see the real me, the me who has no malicious intent or personal agenda other than to get things working properly and help people up their game.

This authenticity makes it easier for me to "connect" with individual stakeholders as fellow human beings and build rapport. The better the rapport, the greater the chances of really getting a handle on people and their true motivations. It's a great conduit for nurturing productive stakeholder relationships. It's also invaluable to get inside individuals' hearts and minds – I've found that what people *really* want or fear isn't always what they say they want or are concerned about.

I was thinking about all this and wondering just what Greg Morgan really wanted as I settled into one of the two chairs in front of his desk, some ten years or so later. In the years since my Electromech PSCM project for Ralph, I had learned a great deal more about handling various stakeholder types effectively, thus expanding my stakeholder management toolkit.

But I never took anything for granted. I always tried to remind myself that every stakeholder is different, as is every work situation or change management project – each one offering the opportunity to practise with the devices in my toolkit or acquire new ones.

I was still in the early years of my career as an independent consultant, and getting a string of assignment successes under my belt was crucial to my long-term career goals. I had to nail this particular assignment to help grow my credibility. But Greg Morgan slightly unsettled me, partly because he remained an enigma. I couldn't tell if he was friend or foe.

Meeting Greg in person for the first time was like meeting a playground legend. The reverberations of his alleged exploits echoed through every area of the company. But you wouldn't have guessed it from the calm atmosphere in his office. I could feel my confidence waver just a tad and tried to pull my mind back to the present moment. After all, this was part of the dance, as experience had taught me. Today's meeting was a key dance move to become au fait with Greg's temperament, and hence how to handle him through this change initiative.

I would have preferred to sit and discuss things at the coffee table in the far corner of his office. But Greg clearly favoured having the discussion while sitting on his throne, a swanky executive leather chair set behind an expansive desk that looked as capacious as the flight deck of an aircraft carrier.

If the size of his desk didn't imprint his importance in the company upon my consciousness, the vast extent of his throne room and its lavish décor certainly hinted at the power and influence he wielded.

Everything about the office screamed Grand Poobah.

Here was a man – no, a pharaoh more like – not to be trifled with. It brought to mind other pharaohs I'd dealt with previously, and I reminded myself that such stakeholders are usually very busy people who guard their time; presiding over an empire, even if it isn't ancient Egypt, is a demanding affair. Such folks can sometimes be brusque or imperious in their manner, which can make them seem uncooperative or quite challenging even though they may not really be. In any case, I had to use my time with him wisely.

"You've got a lovely office here, Greg," I remarked. "I love the nice, open feel."

It was a genuine compliment, not insincere flattery. Although, as I said it, I knew that everyone loves to be praised or admired, and I'd learned to habitually pay tribute to people, sometimes as a way of breaking the ice. I wanted to establish a positive connection immediately and start positioning myself as an ally in his psyche. I knew I had to do this to get to know the Greg Morgan behind the persona and discern as much as possible about his character. What did he really want? What were his true motives? What was his game?

# CHAPTER 5

I HAD BEEN PONDERING THOSE very same questions some days before as I sat at my desk reading an e-mail from Greg. It was addressed to both the Procurement Manager and the Materials Manager – with all the board directors cc'd in, along with several other senior managers whose interests in the matter I couldn't see.

Whenever people choose to communicate like this it always twitches my antenna for organisational politics and Machiavellian tactics.

If you've never worked with colleagues or stake-holders who worship at Machiavelli's altar, then count yourself lucky. And maybe, add to your daily prayers an entreaty that such mercurial characters never cross your career path. But if you've been blessed or cursed – it all depends on how you view things – to have encountered Machiavellian stakeholders in your career, then you'll know that they're typically scheming, duplicitous and unscrupulous types. The sort of characters that'll cause you to sleep with one eye open. You never know when they'll lay a banana skin in your path, thus you can never be too careful in how you proceed.

I couldn't tell if this was the case with Greg. I was too new to the organisation to be sure if this approach of copying in so many people on an e-mail was a deliberate gambit, or just one of his idiosyncrasies, or part of the prevalent culture in the company.

Ribbexo Aerostructures was the jewel in the crown of its parent company, Ribbexo Aerospace Group. The group had been built around the Aerostructures business, which was a very old establishment. And there were vestiges of its antiquated ways apparent to anyone who looked close enough. I was definitely looking. Soaking up the intangible aspects of an organisation, its people and their unspoken manifestations of "how we do things around here" is something that has remained invaluable to me over the years. Because quite often, the attitudes and behaviours of individuals say a lot about the cultural DNA of the wider organisation, and consequently the sorts of stakeholder headaches one might come across.

I had been brought in to help Ribbexo Aerostructures address acute PSCM problems that were crippling the business. Things were so bad that the company was routinely breaching its delivery service-level agreements with customers, and was paying hefty sums in related liquidated damages.

And if that wasn't bad enough, two of their top three customers, who accounted for nearly half the sales revenue, had already given the company penalty cards: if delivery performance didn't improve within six months Ribbexo was on notice of losing the customer business.

I had convinced the CEO, Mark Ryman, to clear his diary for a couple of hours so we could have a lengthy and candid chat when I'd first come on board. A fish rots from the head down, so I always pay close attention to the senior leadership in client organisations. Everything about them – their predispositions, their thinking, their actions, and so on – can often be more revealing than the numbers on a performance scorecard or the fancy words on a website.

I wanted to drill down into Mark's innermost thoughts and feelings to glean some of the unspoken insights and factors pertinent to the PSCM problems.

Greg Morgan turned out to be one of those factors.

In response to my probes, Mark had identified Greg as "the most difficult PSCM stakeholder", saying he was always at war with the Supply Chain team.

Greg was the company's Sales and Marketing Director but apparently felt he should be in Mark's chair running the whole outfit. According to Mark, Greg had even challenged his leadership of the company quite openly in one of the quarterly board meetings with the Group Chief Executive present. He frequently blamed Mark's leadership for the problems the company was facing.

I didn't care about Greg's career ambitions. And I didn't want to get dragged into any rift between him and Mark. Yet it was useful to be aware of both factors. What I primarily cared about was what I was being paid to do: to fix the PSCM problems and get the operation performing robustly. But I was acutely interested in Greg as a character and what he might get up to, because experience had taught me that such stakeholders can make or break any change programme or workplace initiative.

One of the pertinent bits of learning I had consolidated at this stage of my career was the importance of categorising stakeholders according to their interest or stake in one's work, their criticality to one's success, how cooperative they are and the extent of their influence or authority in the organisation – recognising that influence or power doesn't necessarily stem from job title or position.

Some stakeholders will have a high stake in your work activities and the organisational clout to help you succeed or shoot you down; these are key players you must keep sweet and leverage to assure the success of your agenda. Some may not have a high level of interest in your work but still have the power to boost or negate your success; it's wise to build solid relationships with such stakeholders and try to take advantage of their organisational influence to "fly your flag". Other stakeholders will have a key stake in your work but lack the clout to help or hinder your success; it's still prudent to keep them involved and onside as appropriate, and maintain good dialogue with them – these folks can become valuable Supporters especially when things get sticky. And some stakeholders will have no interest in your activities and little or no influence or authority; it's not efficient to waste much effort with this lot, but it's effective to not ignore them completely.

I constantly tried to remind myself to invest more of my stakeholder management efforts where I'd reap the greatest returns. Assessing stakeholders in this way, and crafting my optimal approach accordingly, was always a shrewd exercise that aided my personal effectiveness. It invariably spawned many useful pointers and warning signs. And my appraisal of Greg indicated that I couldn't expect him to become a benign factor in the organisational dynamics just because I had appeared on the scene.

It's always important to understand not just the key players on the field, but the organisational terrain upon which they play their game. It's even more crucial if you really want to get ahead in the organisation, or if your work involves introducing changes in people's working practices and you want to ensure your success. Rather than bumbling through the blind corners and hidden valleys of the terrain, it's far more effective to learn the lay of the land; just as a good hunter tries to know his hunting ground, or a good mountain climber endeavours to learn and respect the mountain terrain. It's all about using your knowledge of the terrain to your advantage.

As a key stakeholder who was allegedly antagonistic towards the Supply Chain team, Greg Morgan was a feature of the terrain I just couldn't ignore.

*

The image of Greg that Mark had given me was confirmed by most of the Supply Chain managers. I had met each of them in introductory one-on-one sessions, and almost every one of them saw Greg as their most difficult stakeholder. Most of them claimed that many of the PSCM problems were actually caused by Greg's salespeople habitually entering sales orders on the Enterprise Resource Planning (ERP) computer system with promised customer delivery dates that flouted the specified product delivery lead times – in effect, causing the PSCM operations to fail right from the get-go.

Some of the Supply Chain managers also shared anecdotes with me of past incidents where Greg had done "his usual thing" of broadcasting "yet another Supply Chain department failure", insinuating that the department managers and staff were incompetent. Apparently, he took every opportunity to discredit the Supply Chain guys, as if he was leading some sort of anti-Supply Chain offensive.

The e-mail I was presently reading, which I had asked the Procurement Manager to forward to me, was a great example of Greg's alleged approach.

Greg had sent the e-mail about a month or two before I came on board. And in that time things had only gone from bad to worse. So he undeniably had more ammunition for his war on Supply Chain. Despite my attempts to read between the lines of the e-mail, I couldn't be sure what the true intent of his campaign was.

In truth, I wasn't expecting to figure out Greg's motives or to get to the core of the PSCM problems purely by deciphering e-mails, like a sorcerer interpreting the divine messages in bones and stones. Engaging him in person would be a key piece of the puzzle.

I had already phoned Greg during my first week at Ribbexo to introduce myself and set up our meeting. He had sounded accommodating. And he'd agreed to see me when he was next on-site the following week. So I only had a few days to wait. For now, I'd have to make do with the perceptions I was building up without jumping to conclusions. I always try to remind myself that things may not always be as they seem, especially when it comes to dealing with wily stakeholders.

The e-mail was never really going to do more than help build those perceptions. I sensed that Greg was a fish who wanted a bigger pond. But was there more to it than his ego and ambition – did he have genuine fears and frustrations about the company's PSCM operations?

I was mulling over this for a number of reasons. I knew there was a risk that Greg could tarnish me with the "incompetent Supply Chain guys" brush, even though I was there to fix things. And if this happened, it would make my job so much harder.

I also knew from bitter experience that sometimes there are some people at work who'll happily see you fail, for all sorts of reasons – it may be because you haven't engaged them tactfully or pandered to their ego; or they think you lack the requisite experience for the job, or you got it because you're pally with some influential person or other; or they're driven by jealousy or their personal agenda; or your failure would take the spotlight off their own incompetence; or they haven't forgiven you for some past slight, which may not have been deliberate on your part; or they don't like your perfume or aftershave; or … God knows what.

Whatever the reasons, stakeholders like this can become a menace to our well-being at work, especially if they deliberately sabotage our efforts.

As yet, I didn't think that Greg would try to derail my work. And my experience with leading various change initiatives had taught me the potential value of stakeholders like him.

All key stakeholders, from the top dog in the big chair to shop-floor operators at the coalface, can hugely enrich the "As-is" picture and improvement efforts on any project or work initiative if their contributions are canvassed sincerely. Capturing stakeholders' inputs often reveals much more about the underlying root causes of organisational problems, because the numbers alone may not tell the full story. I planned to carry out a data-driven root-cause analysis to identify the critical pinch points in Ribbexo's end-to-end supply chain pipeline. But stakeholder views like Greg's would be extremely valuable in helping me grasp the full 360-degree picture.

Getting at that full picture was foremost on my mind, and I tried to avoid letting my initial thoughts about his e-mail cloud my perspective now that I was sitting in front of Greg in his impressive throne room. But I couldn't help wondering: "Is he going to be one of those bloody difficult stakeholders who'll sap my time and energy through unnecessary disagreements, political shenanigans or outright conflicts?"

The quick handshake with which he'd welcomed me into his office hadn't told me much. Neither did his bald pate and rather bland face, which I scrutinised as I watched his body language, something I always pay close attention to when meeting individual stakeholders in person. Reading these countless non-verbal cues can sometimes reveal more than the words people speak.

But reading some people is like reading hieroglyphics. Greg Morgan was one of those. He turned out to be one of the most fascinating characters I've dealt with in my career.

Yes, he was pugnacious and had an ego the size of a planet.

Yes, he was ambitious and hankered after a managing director or CEO role.

And yes, he did think the Supply Chain guys were doing a terrible job and Mark Ryman's interventionist leadership style was part of the problem at Ribbexo.

He was right.

# CHAPTER 6

THAT FIRST MEETING WITH GREG had gone as well as I might have expected. He didn't pull his punches in giving me his views on the PSCM problems and the related organisational factors at play. And he wasn't shy about probing me about my career background, especially my experience with identical PSCM challenges.

I guess he was having an early sniff, checking my groove, and sounding me out to see if I could bring any value or if I might turn out to be a dud.

Greg's sniffing wasn't aberrant behaviour. Your stakeholders do this too. It's part of how they form early impressions, even if it isn't always nor totally done in a conscious way. And it happens quite quickly; we tend to appraise people and make up our minds about them in a few moments – we decide, for instance, whether they're genuine or phoney, whether they're being manipulative or honest with us, or whether we like their groove.

Of course, those initial judgements aren't always correct. But they frequently hold a reasonable dose of accuracy.

With many stakeholders such first impressions can have strong, lasting impacts on how they perceive you and relate to you. Effective stakeholder management intrinsically entails shaping their impressions of you, the work you do, your style or the value you provide. Shifting negative first impressions can be difficult. So starting out with the impression *you* want to give is imperative, as is preserving *la bella figura*. It's a fundamental component of cultivating your personal brand.

I was very conscious of this as I discussed the PSCM issues with Greg, especially as I could sense how difficult a stakeholder he could indeed turn out to be. I knew I couldn't risk offending his sensibilities. I'd have to handle him with kid gloves, and I'd probably need all the "people smarts" in my toolkit and then some.

That toolkit came in very handy in handling not just Greg, but the other senior-level stakeholders in the organisation.

I went to great lengths to woo each of the senior executives, making sure I listened well to what they said and, more importantly, what they didn't say.

And when I presented my findings and improvement recommendations to the board, I made sure my assessment was robust. I included both financial and non-financial considerations in my business case, incorporating a detailed "costs, benefits and risks" analysis. I wanted the message to be about "the business" and its profitability, rather than the technical PSCM issues. And I expressed it in language that would resonate with the board directors. I deliberately made an issue of the business survival risk stemming directly from abysmal performance on customer deliveries. I knew this was an appropriate hook that would capture the directors' attention, especially as their bonuses were tied to the performance of the business. And I knew for sure that I had scored highly with Greg by emphasising the "customer" angle.

When I felt we were at an appropriate stage of the change initiative, I made a point of periodically inviting Greg and one or two of his sales managers to attend our

Supply Chain team meetings. I wanted them to feel that they were part of the wider team trying to improve things, that we were all in it together. And I knew from experience that such inclusive gatherings are an effective way to engender *esprit de corps*.

On these occasions, I'd always allocate time in the meeting agenda for Greg and his guys to give us brief updates on life from their point of view – what was happening in our customer markets, what pains customers were experiencing, any feedback they had on our delivery performance, how well the Supply Chain function was interacting and communicating with the Sales and Marketing folks, and so on.

Aside from the historical failures Greg sometimes dragged up, whenever we dropped the ball during the change programme I was quick to own up and apologise.

Apologising can be difficult for some of us, which is somewhat understandable; no one enjoys being wrong or facing up to their errors. Admitting to someone else that we're wrong or have goofed, and apologising for our blunder, can be even more unpalatable when the person we have to apologise to is a "difficult" colleague or stakeholder.

But apologising sincerely and taking responsibility, without trying to justify one's deeds or oversight, can be quite liberating and even cathartic – perhaps because it frees us from the "prison without walls" we have erected by habitually, though sometimes unknowingly, judging others from atop our moral high horse.

Stepping through the prison gates reminds us that everyone makes mistakes, utters unkind words or behaves in unpleasant ways from time to time, including me, you and our respective stakeholders. Our tendency to criticise, condemn or complain when it comes to others is somewhat hypocritical. And we show our hypocrisy in big and small ways almost every day – such as when we chastise or vilify people who lie to us, yet we lie to ourselves day in, day out; we delude ourselves with all sorts of little white lies about all sorts of things, lies which often hamper us from discovering our best selves and harnessing our mojo. These delusions frequently seem inconsequential at the time we make them. But with the passage of time, they can accumulate and derail us from our path. Little white lies can be greater saboteurs of our career destinies than the worst stakeholder. It's so much better for our success and well-being to face up to our own failings or shortcomings; after all, dropping the ball is part of the human makeup, something our ego often forgets in its chronic self-delusion.

Our ego also forgets that people are likely to accept an apology that is genuine, well timed and expressed with candour. They'll forgive the goof, especially if our subsequent actions back up the apology.

I usually followed up my apology to Greg with clarifying what we were doing to avoid a recurrence of the problem. But I was always careful to avoid the trap of letting my mouth write a bad cheque and promising things I couldn't deliver. If anything, I sometimes deliberately erred on the side of under-promising and over-delivering.

I also tried to speak Greg's lingo as often as possible, whether we were having a formal meeting or an informal corridor conversation. I'd frequently use phrases like "customer delivery performance", for example, or "customer satisfaction", "keeping our customers happy" and "making our Supply Chain organisation more customer-centric". I knew that it made his heart smile to see that *his customers* were at the forefront of my mind. It was a subtle but potent way of increasing my influence with him. And I'm pretty sure my approach made it easy for him to like me and trust me.

Growing my likeability and trust capital with Greg were two effects I valued deeply. Like two precious condiments that brought nourishment, good flavour and everything desirable to the essence of our relationship. If people like you, they're more likely to develop positive notions of your personal brand, and they're more likely to want to work with you harmoniously and productively. And if people trust you, that likelihood increases exponentially. Because trust is the unspoken bond that is foundational to all healthy relationships, a priceless asset that isn't always easy to acquire yet is so easy to lose.

Strengthening my relationship bond with Greg could only bring good fortune.

This specific dynamic between us was particularly helpful when it came to fixing one of the two biggest factors at the root of Ribbexo's PSCM problems.

*

The root-cause analysis I had carried out had confirmed the anecdotal evidence from the Supply Chain guys that Greg's salespeople were a huge part of the PSCM problems. It was impossible for Greg himself to deny it when I presented him with my audit findings, based on hard data from the company's ERP computer system over a significant time period – including minute details like the date and time a particular problem sales order was entered on the system, which of his salespeople had created it, how the order had then progressed through the supply chain pipeline, all the way through to being delivered late to the customer.

The data didn't lie. It told a damning story. And pinpointed the systemic issues putting Ribbexo's survival at stake.

Greg and I both knew his guys had to be more disciplined with customer sales orders by adhering to the company's defined product delivery lead times.

I deliberately didn't make a song and dance about "the sales orders issue" – with him or anyone else. Bad-mouthing stakeholders just doesn't contribute anything positive to the relationship.

It can be very tempting to say disparaging or scornful things about an individual stakeholder or a group of stakeholders, or to ridicule or stigmatise them in some other way, especially if you're having difficulties with them. But it's probably best to not give in to the temptation.

That's not to say you can't or shouldn't discuss your difficulties with trusted colleagues, friends or family members. Getting things off your chest or venting into a listening ear can be helpful to relieve emotional pressure, and getting some perspective from others can expand your perceptions and understanding and aid your capacity to deal with the difficulty more effectively. Such exchanges may be good for your mojo, when the discussion isn't centred on poisoning the air with words that harm another human spirit – which is what bad-mouthing is; a toxic and infectious activity that erodes your credibility and integrity as a professional. It hurts the reputation of your stakeholder. And in the long run, it'll hurt yours too and damage your personal brand. It definitely doesn't help you nurture sound stakeholder relationships.

For similar reasons, I never rubbed Greg's nose in it either – despite the fact that he hadn't mentioned his empire as a culprit when he'd highlighted the organisational factors pertinent to the PSCM problems to me. And I wouldn't condone the Supply Chain guys gloating over Greg's people being "caught out". Making them feel cornered would do nothing to help but everything to hinder. A cornered animal has nothing to lose and will come out fighting; its defensive bite could turn out to be your worst nightmare.

When we gloat over stakeholders' misfortunes, call them out publicly when it's inappropriate or make them feel trapped, all we're doing is causing umbrage and sowing fertile seeds of resentment, malice and enmity. Those seeds will sprout. When you least expect. They'll catch you unawares with unwelcome consequences like the bite of the cornered animal.

I knew that to plant seeds of success it'd be more prudent to be gracious with Greg and his guys, just as the gods show us all divine grace over our daily transgressions. So I just treated the sales orders issue as one of the root-cause factors to be fixed, prioritising it as a biggie.

I dug into my toolkit yet again to get Greg's salespeople to change their behaviours and comply with the product lead-time stipulations.

One of the devices I extracted was to leverage Greg himself to help achieve this, because people dance to the tune of their leaders. Trying to achieve behavioural change with the salespeople without their pharaoh's support would be like chasing pavements that lead nowhere.

Reaching out to Greg for help and engaging his support probably augmented our alignment. Because there's something in the human spirit that enjoys helping other humans and gains some sort of fulfilment from it, like an evolutionary instinct to promote collective human welfare by giving help to another. As if we know, somewhere deep down in our souls, that despite the endless momentum of events and busyness we're subject to, when we give we also get our share – a share of something that may not always be tangible, something we may not even be conscious of, something that may be ineffable. But we know it feels good.

Studies have proved that helping others or an act of kindness gives us an uplifting feeling, a sense of satisfaction, a degree of happiness and well-being described by Allan Luks as "Helper's High".

Perhaps I was giving Greg's spirit a high by enlisting his help.

Or perhaps I was providing soul food for him to feed his karma.

Or maybe I was just appealing to his self-interest in not wanting himself or his people to continue to look bad now that the can of worms sat open under a microscope.

Whatever the case, my device undeniably aided my efforts to attune him to my groove.

It must have helped, too, that whenever we were engaged in conversation, I made a point of saying his name, "Greg", frequently without sounding like a parrot. It was another subtle way of fostering affinity with him. As Dale Carnegie pointed out in his renowned book, a person's name is indeed the most beautiful sound they ever hear. Calling a stakeholder by name in discussions can be a powerful way of attuning them at a subconscious level.

If that sounds too simple, remember that sometimes in life the simple, little things yield the most remarkable effects – little things like a genuine smile, a few kind words or being fully present and attentive.

The challenge for some of us, especially when we're inundated with the innumerable demands of our busyness or the routine pressures of work, is that the human mind has a propensity to be everywhere but where it should be most: here, in the present, right now, this moment. This affliction of *la tête ailleurs* is what prevails when we're thinking about our response to what a stakeholder is saying rather than totally focusing on what is being said and how it is being conveyed to us. It inhibits our ability to pay full attention to the simple, little things right in front of us, things that often shape the cadence of our day-to-day interactions with stakeholders.

# CHAPTER 7

GREG WAS A MUST-WIN STAKEHOLDER and the onus was on me to keep him onside. I made concerted efforts to empathise with him and stroke his ego, while treating his views and concerns with priority. He certainly had something to bring to the party. His role at the front end of the business, his position at the top table and his long tenure with the company all made him a treasure trove of priceless insights into Ribbexo's PSCM problems.

Greg also made several worthwhile suggestions on shaping the change programme. For instance, I remember when I was planning a series of company-wide town hall briefings to communicate the challenge we were facing and share our planned improvement approach. These briefings were a key aspect of a broader drive to engage stakeholders, solicit their views and inputs, and engender buy-in. In essence, I was expanding the collaborative approach I had adopted with the Sales and Marketing guys – we *really* were all in it together; because we all worked for the same company and if we didn't fix the systemic problems I had unearthed, the consequences for everyone in the company could be dire. Yet the rewards could be fabulous if we triumphed.

I wanted the town hall briefings to touch every department and involve staff at all levels, from the board directors down to the shop-floor operators, in mixed groups. I mentioned my intent to Greg in one of our weekly catch-up sessions.

"That's a good idea, Sigi," he said.

"Thanks Greg," I responded. "I have to confess though, I'm struggling a bit with developing a briefing schedule that will cover everyone without creating too much disruption or bringing the company to a standstill."

He didn't reply directly or add anything specific to his earlier comment, and we moved on to discuss other issues.

Much to my surprise, a couple of days or so later Greg rang me and offered to help me out. We put our heads together and came up with a schedule that was as good as, if not better than, anything I could have put together on my own. He undoubtedly saved me a few hours' head-scratching.

On another occasion, when we'd been making noticeable headway with slaying the systemic problem issues, I wanted to capture some stakeholder views on our progress – through a series of structured interviews – for a very specific purpose. Greg agreed to be interviewed. And during the interview, he gave me some particular examples of positive changes he had observed and provided a glowing endorsement of "the reformed Supply Chain department", as he put it.

The interview and the town hall briefings schedule were just two of a number of inputs from Greg which I greatly appreciated. Ultimately, he turned out to be an invaluable contributor to the change initiative.

Admittedly, it took considerable patience and dexterity on my part to tease out and harness his contribution. It was certainly no piece of cake. There were several occasions when I was sorely tempted to use my voodoo magic powers to cast evil spells on him.

I think I only kept my sanity by staying focused on my objectives, and constantly reminding myself of all the stuff I had learned from previous stakeholder challenges.

Dealing with Greg was like dancing with angels and demons. The times when his involvement seemed so favourable it felt like divine intervention were offset by the moments when he seemed a damn nuisance.

In those times when he jangled my nerves and I really wished I could shut him up momentarily or switch him off completely, I reminded myself that humans are not like computers or light switches that one can simply turn on and turn off. We're not wholly rational; we're complex beings, with behaviours that can sometimes be idiosyncratic, induced by a blend of personal, psychological and environmental influences – a blend that is so complicated it has spawned numerous professions, thousands of university faculties and millions of specialists across the world, just to get a handle on this one species called "human".

The personal factors that sometimes impel our behaviours are things like age, gender, marital status, education and religious beliefs. The psychological influences include personality types, attitudes and values. And the environmental factors are things like political orientations, financial or economic circumstances and social and cultural norms. With this composite soup of influences, it's no surprise that dealing with some humans can sometimes feel like handling jelly.

On top of that, we're also driven by so many visible and invisible forces – like the defined work processes we follow, the problems and struggles we're living through, or the emotions coursing through our spirit at any point in life. For instance, a stakeholder going through a bitter divorce may not be the most agreeable person to work with at the time. Nor would a stakeholder facing severe health problems or contending with some other traumatic circumstances, or one desperately trying to quit smoking, perhaps.

So it's always helpful to remember that when a colleague or stakeholder comes across as "difficult", quite often there's a lot more going on below the surface. You may not ordinarily know what exactly but you get the vibe.

In the same way, our own psychological and physiological states deeply affect the impressions we form about things, people, events or experiences. This has a relationship to our sentiments, attitudes, internal dialogue or self-talk, and our actions. It colours most aspects of our lives, including our work, in substantial ways which many of us are unaware of. And somewhat unsurprisingly, all of this affects the way *we* come across to others.

Just as you may perceive a stakeholder's vibe, you're also giving off a vibe of your own, which individual stakeholders pick up on and react to. How you yourself are feeling – angry, frustrated, stressed out, nervous, optimistic, inspired or calmly confident – will almost always impact how you interact with your stakeholders and how they'll come across to you.

To me, Greg Morgan came across as a conundrum of sorts. He certainly wasn't trying to quit smoking. And he wasn't divorcing his wife either. I wasn't always able to gauge what he was feeling or thinking. But reminding myself that he was *a human being*, and thus could be subject to any number of myriad challenges and influences in his personal and professional life, helped keep me away from the voodoo doll.

Another reminder I entrenched in my thinking is that an "organisation" is a collection of individuals pursuing a common purpose in an "organised" manner. Therefore, every individual in the organisation has a role to play, whether or not they're sly foxes, gentle lambs or dominant bruisers in temperament. Appreciating each other's roles, personalities and related expectations and imbibing that understanding to our approach in our work aids the smooth running of the organisation.

I had definitely put considerable effort into getting a good grasp of Greg's expectations. As regards PSCM, all he'd ever really wanted was to keep his customers happy – quite understandable for a sales and marketing director – rather than the immense customer dissatisfaction he'd constantly had to deal with.

But no one had previously done a structured and thorough root-cause analysis to show him that he could go a long way to achieve his desire by addressing issues within his own empire. Perhaps because no one had the toolkit I'd brought with me to Ribbexo, a toolkit that contained several devices to stop people playing the blame game; because indulging in finger-pointing with stakeholders is as useful as planting seeds of grass to grow a field of roses.

My efforts to keep Greg informed, involved and onside throughout the assignment paid off handsomely. He became one of the key Supporters of the change programme, which proved a fantastic success not just for the Supply Chain team but for the broader Ribbexo business.

To top it all off, Greg wrote me a wonderful testimonial for my business website after I completed the assignment. Not bad for someone who was deemed "the most difficult stakeholder".

# A THOUSAND POUNDS
# OF STRESS

# CHAPTER 8

IF GREG MORGAN WASN'T THE most difficult stakeholder, then Dickhead John undoubtedly qualified for that crown.

I knew it in that moment, way back then, as I stood staring at him in shock. I could easily have strangled him right there and then. I had a strong urge to do something dastardly that'd leave him in no doubt about the rage that was engulfing me.

I stood there for a minute trying hard to calm myself and reminding myself to breathe deeply and slowly. I was struggling though. All the pent-up negative emotions

I'd been carrying for weeks on end threatened to burst through and unleash something I'd probably regret.

In hindsight, I think John himself would have regretted it too, though it may have taken him longer to face up to the truth. I'm sure he'd have found it difficult to admit to himself that he'd been a constant thorn in my side since I started this job. And this time he had crossed a line.

I had arrived at work very early that morning as usual. Getting in a couple of hours before the work day began and staying back as late as nine o'clock at night had become standard for me. I had so much to do. And occasionally I felt overwhelmed, as if this time I had bitten off more than I could chew.

I knew I could do it. But I was struggling to move from firefighting mode to fire prevention. Problems of all sorts seemed to crop up every single day, from supplier failures holding up key projects to major disciplinary issues in the team I had inherited. My e-mail inbox looked like a garbage dump in a third-world country. I was run ragged trying to put out so many fires burning all at once. And more and more, it was starting to look as if John was the chief arsonist. He was also often the first one to shout "Fire! Fire!"

Those few hours early in the morning and late in the evening were about the only time I was able to do productive work that would get me out of firefighting. I wasn't just motivated by my desire for a saner, more effective work life; deep down in my soul, a part of me harboured a fear that I'd be sacked. I don't know how I'd have coped with that.

I knew that my boss, Layla Patterson, thought highly of me. In fact, it was the reason she had appointed me to the role in the first place. But I also knew that she wouldn't sacrifice her reputation for me.

Layla was the regional Vice President of Operations in Europe for Tempura Products Inc., a mid-market supplier of high-technology electronic products for the automotive, telecoms and consumer electronics sectors. I'd known her name as a big kahuna in the regional organisation when I first joined the company. Back then I had been recruited to set up a Strategic Supplier Management function, which ended up comprising just me. Despite this handicap, I had made a success of the role and got myself noticed by some of the top brass. But what I really wanted was to move into a line management role, and preferably one with high visibility and impact.

I wanted to make a name for myself to assure my career growth in the company.

That desire was what drove me to seize the moment when Tempura went through a redundancy programme a couple of years later. I knew that most of my colleagues spent those unsettling days worrying about their job security. I chose to spend the time scanning the environment and quietly approaching a few big cheeses to see what opportunities the redundancy programme might throw up for me. I suspected that the company would use the redundancies to get rid of dead wood and put more effective people in key roles.

Layla was one of the senior executives I approached to discuss my career aspirations and explore possible job openings in her area.

When she eventually told me that she'd like to appoint me to lead the Product Supply Network (PSN) team, my first reaction was to ask about John Reed, the incumbent PSN Manager. But she was reticent and talked about the department itself instead. She indicated that she was wholly dissatisfied with the department's performance, that it seemed to be festooned with all manner of problems and she was constantly dealing with escalations and negative feedback from stakeholder departments.

She portrayed a picture of bedlam in the entire product supply operations, with rampant disorderliness, shoddy practices and weak governance. She said, basically, she wanted me to "get in there and sort the place out".

I remember asking her a number of key questions that I felt were very pertinent. For example, I asked about the job description; there was none. I asked about the defined objectives and key performance indicators for the role and the department; there were none – she said John occasionally gave her reports on specific projects but she was never really able to make sense of them. My questions about departmental processes, systems and tools were just as fruitless. As were my probes about the employees in the team.

We eventually agreed when my appointment would be announced and when I'd start the job.

I was so delighted to have secured the line management role I'd hankered after, I drove home on cloud nine that evening. The fact that I had got the job through my own initiative, and that I had read the organisational situation correctly and taken advantage of it, was even more thrilling.

But I knew that I'd be on trial, so to speak. If the PSN department was as dysfunctional as Layla had stated, then the spotlight would be on me for sure. I'd have to deliver.

I spent the period before my start date refreshing my knowledge on best practices in product supply management, and working out the most effective way to embark on this new career move. Tempura was a mature company that had evolved in various ways over many decades, and it was filled with many old-timers who'd been there man and boy. Most of these guys viewed new entrants like me as young whippersnappers who lacked the familiarity and supposed superior knowledge they had acquired from their forever-and-a-day tenures. They typically spoke and acted like they were the elite, the chosen ones who really had a good understanding of the business. They'd probably be shocked at my appointment. I knew that, as well as delivering on the job, it was imperative that I displayed the right comportment.

In those few days before I started – and well into my first couple of months or so – I kept reminding myself to listen more and talk less as I engaged with various stakeholders, because my initial intent was to learn and understand as much as possible without prejudging.

I'd have to keep an open mind while soaking up all the factual and anecdotal information available.

I also knew that I'd have to uncover a lot of things myself, especially the unsavoury stuff. And I expected some.

If the department was grossly underperforming then there had to be many things being done wrong, just as there'd be many wrong things being done. And such problems typically come down to people; because, ultimately, it's people that create performance, good or bad. Those same people, within and outside the department, are unlikely to fess up voluntarily, saying, "Hey Sigi, here's such and such problem I created because …" I'd have to probe for details to help me gather insights, using as much open questioning as possible, without making anyone feel accused or under attack. This would require more than maintaining candour on my part. I'd also need to curtail some of my own enthusiasm and avoid shooting from the hip, keep a cool head, and try to be mature and keep my focus on the issues that really mattered.

More than anything else, I wanted to maintain a "confidence without arrogance" attitude and feel comfortable in my own skin, that sublime yet sometimes elusive state the French call *bien dans sa peau*.

It was all good preparation for a new job, especially one that involved new stakeholders all round.

But it was inadequate preparation for possibly the most important thing of all.

# CHAPTER 9

As I HAD AGREED WITH Layla, I set up an initial meeting with John to commence a handover of the department. He sounded quite okay with it all when we spoke on the phone. He even said he was looking forward to helping me find my feet in the job.

"What a wonderful start!" I thought to myself as I put the phone down.

Little did I know that John's apparent cooperation was a charade that masked an impending onslaught of acrimony.

The first telltale signs started to emerge during the series of discussions we had as part of the handover. He wasn't particularly forthcoming with key information and was quite vague in his answers to many of my questions. It felt like pulling teeth sometimes.

I'd frequently use direct or explicit questions like, "When was Gavin Smith's last performance appraisal?"; or, "Are there any other issues with this supplier, no matter how minor, which you haven't mentioned?"; or, "When is the next phase review meeting for XYZ project?", and he'd still be cagey or evasive in his answers.

Misinformation or giving a partial picture on things like the location of the stationery cupboard is one thing. But when it's crucial stuff, like the status of business-critical projects, approval documents for key suppliers, disciplinary issues with staff, or delivery dates for high-risk material supplies, that's something else entirely.

My intuition was whispering to me that something wasn't right, that John wasn't as supportive as he claimed to be and there was some impalpable undercurrent of ill will. But I didn't heed its signal. Not then anyway. I was relying too much on the rationality that goes hand in hand with my five senses, especially my sight – something we all do reflexively, probably way too often; and probably because "seeing is believing".

Yet believing can also result in seeing.

And some of the most important things in life cannot be seen. Like the air we breathe that keeps us alive; the thoughts, emotions and impulses we experience that often drive our actions, and hence shape our lives; and the thing we feel inside when we snuggle up to our loved ones. They're invisible to our eyes yet they exist.

Of course, you should trust your eyes, but remember that they can deceive you. So never rely entirely on your eyes or your five senses alone. What you perceive inside – your sixth sense, intuition, gut instinct, your inner "silent knowledge" or call it what you will – can be indicating valuable truths that your eyes or your rational faculties can't detect or fathom.

You may be wondering what ethereal concepts like intuition and gut instinct have to do with business or work issues, and specifically managing stakeholders. If you continue on the path that led you to reading this story, I suspect that, like me, at some point on your career adventure you'll eventually discover the tremendous value of tapping into the silent knowledge of your inner guru.

Your inner guru is a phenomenal companion that can help you rock to a sweeter tempo. It's an aide that is relied upon by many of the most successful people in all walks of life, people who are wiser, more experienced and more accomplished than me.

It's quite easy to validate this for yourself, by picking a few such people and asking them.

Or, better still, look at yourself. Think how often you use this inner silent knowledge *almost every day* without questioning. For instance, when you "just know, somehow" that something isn't quite right with your child. Or when you "can just tell" that your spouse or your close friend is unsettled or deeply unhappy even when their outward behaviour is normal. Or when you sense that your mistress or your fancy man is lying to you. You're using this capacity in your private life already without trying to reason out *how* you know what you know. So why not bring it to work with you?

For most of my own career, I've often taken my inner guru to work with me without realising I was doing so. But I haven't always been able to tune in properly, partly because, like many of us at work, I'd get buffeted or bamboozled by the "noise" – the organisational ineffectiveness and the games people play, people like John Reed.

The ability to fade out the noise and tune into yourself, or listen to your inner guru, is greatly undervalued amongst the arsenal of skills the modern-day professional

requires for workplace success. It's a fundamental requirement for effective self-leadership.

Many of us instinctively think "leadership" is exclu-
sively about managing others. Yet our ability to manage
ourselves as individuals is just as impactful on our work
success. If you can't manage yourself effectively, how can
you possibly manage your interactions with any stakeholder or the relationship you have with them?

If you cultivate the habit of spending time with your
inner guru, looking under the hood and getting your
house in order, over time you'll be astounded at how
much wisdom lies dormant within you. And this is vital
for your workplace success, because, more than anyone
else, you have the greatest stake in your work – you are
your number-one stakeholder, numero uno.

If you don't cultivate the habit, you'll frequently end
up reacting to outside events, circumstances or people,
rather than responding with self-assurance. You could
become an unwitting puppet to external factors pulling
your strings.

John was certainly doing a great job of pulling my
strings. And despite the whispers of my inner guru, my
logical or rational self just couldn't discern what he was up
to. He was knowingly spinning a web of disinformation

and confusion around me in a devious attempt to make me look ill-informed and incompetent.

His efforts weren't limited to holding back key data from me or passing on misleading information. He was constantly poking his fingers in everywhere, covertly, acting as if he was still in charge of the department. He made decisions on departmental issues behind my back and never even bothered to say a word to me. But he definitely said a few derogatory words about me to others, as I found out later. On several occasions, I'd turn up to a meeting with other stakeholder groups and learn that John had given them direction on some departmental matter or another. Or I'd find out that one of my team was working on some nonsensical task that John had just assigned them, or, worse, that he had instructed them to stop an activity I'd asked them to carry out.

And all this was happening while John categorically continued to give me the impression that he was now fully "hands-off". He constantly asserted that "It's all yours now, Sigi. You're in charge … I'm no longer involved …" This had lately become his typical answer whenever I asked for his opinion or assistance on some issue with historical antecedents.

It was all very infuriating.

And it felt like some endless aggravation that I'd inherited with the job, except it wasn't in the verbal job description Layla had given me.

\*

John still reported to Layla. But he had been sidelined into a newly created, inconsequential "Process and Systems" role, while I had taken over his previous job – a role which was of considerably more importance.

As a technology products business, new products and upgrades to existing products were the lifeblood of Tempura's continued prosperity. Thus, the manufacturing and supply logistics of these product portfolio enhancements were accorded high importance across the organisation, right up to the executive board. It followed that the related functional areas were also renowned. And a department like PSN, which was responsible for pilot projects to define the production and distribution network for all products, was always in the spotlight. So, invariably, whoever occupied the departmental big chair was deemed "important" – no matter how inept the particular individual might be.

This aggregate outlook pervaded the organisation. It partly manifested in the unwillingness to challenge "important" individuals who were crap at their jobs, especially in a culture where old-timers were esteemed more for their time served than their tangible contributions to the business. In many senses, it was a form of the organisational malady popularised by Irving Janis's research as "groupthink", where the desire for conformity or harmony amongst individuals hampers the effectiveness and performance of the collective. This ailment is sometimes at the root of the problems we encounter with stakeholders – their inclinations may be mirroring what's pervasive across the organisation.

This organisational climate suited John perfectly. He was one of those managers who'd been in the company since the Devil was a baby. That's why he was able to get away with his antics. You'd think that somebody somewhere would have said something along the lines of, "… sorry, John, that's a decision for Sigi, as he's now the PSN Manager …", or, "… thanks for your input, John, but we can't act on that, we'll get Sigi's instruction instead …"

The collective acceptance of John's interference was like kindling that stoked my infuriation.

But maybe I should have seen all this coming. It's possible that would have saved me some torment. And it might have helped prevent the fury that was now surging through me, threatening to erupt like a pent-up volcano, as I faced John across his desk while still struggling to stay calm and keep breathing deeply and slowly.

Thank God my efforts paid off. There'd be no dastardly act on my part, and no gruesome fate for him. And there'd be no police cars or ambulances arriving at Tempura that day to cart one or both of us off. But there was no denying that John had indeed crossed a line, and I wasn't going to let it go. Instructing my team to relocate their desks to an entirely different location on the site – for no apparent reason other than he knew he could get away with it because they wouldn't dare disobey – was stark lunacy. Doing it while I was away for a couple of days at another Tempura facility was almost sinister.

Clearly, he wasn't just trying to trip me up; he was dedicated to making me fail and was relentless in pursuing his goal, like a fanatical crusader waging a holy war.

The full realisation dawned on me as I stood there listening to his reason for his latest stunt.

"As a senior manager in the Operations area, I have a responsibility to make sure the teams are working well. And I think your team shouldn't be sitting close to the Production Planning and Control guys so they don't distract them …" he prattled on, without an ounce of conviction.

Of course, it was complete hogwash. I was no longer blinded by his words. And I knew in that moment of epiphany that it was time to change gear with John.

# CHAPTER 10

ALTHOUGH I HADN'T INITIALLY APPRECIATED it, John's crusade was somewhat imaginable.

Logic or rational reasoning would dictate that he had no grounds to make my life hell since I hadn't done anything to him. It wasn't as if he had lost his prestigious job because of me, or I'd been the one who put his nose out of joint by ousting him from the role. But trying to grasp people issues purely from a logical standpoint is like chaining yourself to a madman.

The loss of face John felt had clearly unleashed a torrent of bitterness that was powerful enough to compel the spite he directed at me.

Sometimes, dealing with extremely perverse stakeholder behaviour like this can be the gateway to a pilgrimage of learning and self-discovery. In my case, one of the first learning points was acknowledging my failure to *adequately* consider John's likely feelings of humiliation – in my preparations for the job, I should have given more regard to his emotions about losing his highly esteemed job to a supposedly inexperienced upstart like me. It was a cardinal error. Because the circumstances in which the management change had occurred meant that, for a while at least, John was my most important stakeholder in many senses, and certainly one to be handled deftly. I only had myself to blame for the vitriolic deluge of jealousy, envy and resentment his defenestration had spouted, which was now threatening to drown me.

If you venture into the jungle without adequate preparation, you can't blame anyone else for whatever ills befall you. This sort of self-honesty, rather than self-pity, is what a pilgrimage is about.

The acknowledgement of my own failure was far more important than dealing with John's antics. Being forced into my firefighter's outfit, playing catch-up to an arsonist who was brilliant with matches, was the price I paid for that blunder.

John's constant interference, his deceit and the innumerable problems he'd been causing me had made me start to loathe him. Time and time again, I'd found myself thinking, "What a dickhead!" Which is exactly how I'd started to truly feel about him – he was no longer John Reed in my mind, he had become "Dickhead John". And that's how I referred to him whenever I was recounting one of his latest exploits to my wife.

Dickhead John had become a challenge that proved as daunting as the new job itself.

A challenge can be an insurmountable problem, if you view it as such. Or it can be a mere difficulty which can be overcome, if you're a bit more conscious and determined. It can even be an opportunity – an opportunity for growth; if you're savvy enough to see through the noise and remember that we only grow when we stretch beyond what we can do already. And what you learn from such challenges at work becomes a gift.

I had been trying desperately to recognise the learning opportunity in the situation with John. I kept forcing myself to examine "me" – my mindset, my feelings, my approach, my perspectives, and so on. I'd say to myself several times, "Sigi, are you sure John is the problem? Are you sure you're not overreacting? …"

I also contemplated whether I had always encountered the exact same problems previously. It's a critical consideration to grow one's effectiveness. If you keep facing the same issues with different colleagues and stakeholders or in different situations, then maybe you should stop and recognise the common factor in these occurrences: you. Is life trying to tell you something? It could be there's something you need to learn from these repeated experiences.

In the same vein, I considered whether I had experienced such difficulties with the *same type* of stakeholder in the past. Recalling past experiences can sometimes be helpful in dealing with the present and preparing for the future. But one must always be careful not to dwell in the past; the present is far more important. The sages repeatedly remind us of the power of the present in the tapestry of life because it's in the present moment that the past is entwined with the future – each moment of life is a gap between what went before and what is to come. So the past and the future are interlinked by our thoughts, feelings, awareness and actions in the current moment.

Reflecting on the past, the desired future and your current dispositions, without getting trapped in any negative emotions or pessimistic thoughts, helps you remain the puppet master.

When I was reflecting on some specific misdeed John had committed which had left me seething, I'd force myself to examine my interpretation of the particular circumstances. In situations like these, asking yourself critical questions can often prove insightful – questions like: Do you really have indisputable proof that your take on things is precisely correct and faultless? Could there possibly, even if not probably, be an alternative and equally valid angle? How will your success, or, perish the thought, your failure, at the job or task impact the other person's? If someone else was in this situation, what advice would you give them?

These sorts of self-enquiries are particularly relevant when we're caught up in the wild flames of thoughts and emotions that typically accompany such terrible stakeholder experiences. And even more so when we're unaware of the undercurrent of those sentiments in our psyche.

I was very aware of the current of emotions threatening to sweep me up as I grappled with John and his devilry. My self-enquiries weren't just the ruminations of a man losing his mind, although John was doing a good job of driving me mad. These were valuable deliberations that helped me better understand myself, how I relate to others and my approach to workplace challenges.

Importantly, regularly scheduling time in my week to sit still and have meetings with myself, where these considerations poured forth, gave me much-needed refuge from the maelstrom of work difficulties I was grappling with.

This habit of carving out time to scrutinise myself and consider things properly, through the prism of "life and learning", helped me curb the tendency to run with my first thoughts or react to events impulsively. Our reflexive views or judgements may sometimes be right but don't always lead to the best decisions in all contexts. And our instantaneous discernments may be tainted by our cognitive biases – the distorted patterns of reasoning and decision-making, developed over time, which unconsciously influence our judgement and can blind us to new insights, leading to flawed choices.

The practice of quiet rumination and tapping the sage wisdom of your inner guru will prove a real boon in handling your own stakeholder challenges. And more importantly, it'll help you become aware of who you truly are, what you stand for, how you think and act, and why you think and act the way you do.

This self-insight will steer you towards the best in you and help you sing the song in your heart with verve and gusto.

I was determined that John wouldn't silence my song. But the tough situation at work meant that on many occasions I was only able to make "guru time" at weekends. It was a bit of a sacrifice. But the gift that eventually emerged was worth it; the prize was way beyond the price.

However, discovering that gift required overcoming a significant amount of anguish, self-doubt and performance anxiety, with a sprinkling of self-criticism thrown in just to spice things up.

Some of these sorts of revelations sometimes emerge when we face up to our "shadow self": the aggregation of those aspects of our personality which we typically reject or choose to ignore, often because we find them undesirable. Interestingly, we may recognise a few of these same traits *in others*, not least some of the stakeholders or work colleagues we view as "difficult". As many psychologists attest, Carl Jung was quite canny in asserting that "Everything that irritates us about others can lead us to an understanding of ourselves."

The irksome foibles you see in others can act as a mirror or a beam of light to help you learn to face up to your shadow, which provides an unparalleled depth of self-awareness and helps you manage yourself better. This self-management is priceless when dealing with troublesome stakeholders, especially malevolent ones like John.

\*

My deep reflections about the situation with John and his crusade of sabotage had led me to try out various ways of handling him. I had tried to be conciliatory, deliberately avoiding butting heads with him. I'd often found the friendly approach quite effective with most stakeholders. And I knew that open hostilities can lead to unintended consequences, if not outright calamity.

People often feel under attack when confronted head-on, even when presented with glaring evidence of their transgressions or the untenable nature of their positions. It's one of the reasons to avoid trying to "win" an argument with a stakeholder in a conventional sense; they're quite likely to feel threatened or dig their heels in. It's often more effective to approach their contention with respect and consideration, acknowledging any positive points therein, before presenting them with the logical or probable outcomes of their position.

I had been mindful of this in my dealings with John so far. I had also been deliberate at trying to exploit humour and laughter in our interactions. I knew that humour is a powerful weapon of the human soul, a bequest from the gods which we receive at birth. It's one of the richest and freshest ingredients in the alchemy of healthy human interactions. Injecting appropriate doses of humour into your stakeholder relationships – whether to break the ice initially, to smoothen ruffled feathers or to keep the vibe sweet – is one of the easiest ways to get in your groove at work.

Admittedly, it may be easier for extroverts than introverts, or those with charisma or chutzpah. Also, it could be less effective with stakeholders of a dispassionate temperament. And as you'd expect, not everyone will get your humour. But it's still worth trying, as I did with John.

I used humour and other tactful approaches I judged to be appropriate, both publicly and in our private discussions – aside from the formal one-on-one meetings we'd held during the handover transition, I continued to meet him privately; usually in his office, so he could feel more at ease being on his home turf.

Whether I was meeting him in an attempt to break bread or to investigate another arson attack, these discussions had proved as fruitless as all my other approaches so far. On the few occasions I had momentarily felt successful in my endeavours to get John onside, he always did something sooner rather than later to shatter my illusions. It made me feel like Sisyphus, repeatedly pushing a huge boulder up a mountain only for it to roll back down every time it nears the summit.

But life has a way of unwrapping its gifts to us in its own perfect time, *tempo giusto*. My gift had been emerging even before I realised it.

My recognition of the need to shift gears with John reflected my emergent growth. And making the decision in that moment – as I listened to him – changed the tapestry of our future relationship. I was reclaiming the puppet master's chair. Moreover, I would do it assertively, in a professional and dignified manner. It was time to discard my firefighter garb and put on my gladiator outfit with special armour plating, cloaked under a pinstripe suit.

I let him finish spouting his baloney about relocating my team.

"Sorry, John, what you're saying doesn't make any sense at all. It sounds like total bunkum to me," I replied, keeping my voice calm but firm.

He tried to interrupt me but I continued speaking without hesitation, in a reasonable and clear tone. "Your actions are extremely unprofessional and wholly unacceptable. You're not responsible for the PSN department, and you have no right to move my team or to interfere in any way at all. I want you to be crystal clear about this: if anything like this happens again, I'll be pursuing the matter formally with HR."

I turned around and walked out of his office, leaving him standing there looking like he'd been visited by the Four Horsemen of the Apocalypse.

I don't think anyone in the company had given it to him straight like that before.

But I wasn't done. Bearding this lion required more assertive actions.

I went over to see our HR Business Partner, and asked her if she knew anything about the relocation of my team. She didn't. She seemed perplexed by the notion of such a thing happening without my involvement and authorisation. I got a similar reaction from the Facilities Manager responsible for our area of the site when I spoke to him straight afterwards.

I went back to my office, closed the door and stood by the window for a few minutes, focusing my attention on the in-and-out flow of my breath. I wanted to be clear-headed and emotionally solid for my next action. I knew it'd be dangerous and unproductive to respond to the situation or take action in the throes of being upset or angry. Such incidences can bring out the worst in us or make us feel vengeful. But a desire for vengeance can blind you.

The longer I stood there, the more I could feel the gentle current of my breathing, like a soft summer breeze that soothed my spirit, blowing away a thousand pounds of stress that John had heaped on me since I took over the job.

When I felt ready, I sat at my desk to craft a couple of e-mails. I deliberately took my time to think through my message and choose my words carefully. This was way too important to allow myself to fall for the traps that frequently ensnare many of us when we communicate by e-mail.

I'm not a big fan of e-mail as a primary form of communication with stakeholders. You can't engage with people via e-mail the way you can face to face. And you can't read an e-mail like you can read a person. That's why I prefer to interact with stakeholders in person whenever possible and appropriate.

Naturally, some people prefer to have information conveyed by e-mail. So I try to stay flexible. I always ask myself what medium of communication will be most effective in achieving the outcomes I want.

Sometimes the practicality of the situation outweighs the desire for optimum engagement effectiveness; one must not let the perfect be an enemy of the good. Dealing with stakeholders in a different location, especially in another country, is one such example. It's a challenge that cripples many stakeholder management endeavours. You can easily become overdependent, knowingly or not, on e-mail communication to manage such stakeholders. Experience has taught me that this may not be productive a lot of the time, especially when you're trying to win over critical stakeholders or keep them onside – it's nigh on impossible to do this *effectively* while perpetually hiding behind your desk or your e-mails; you've got to eyeball key stakeholders every so often, even if it's just via a video call at the very least.

Thankfully, with modern technology you can still sit at your desk and make those video calls so your stakeholders can see your sparkle.

Of course, if, like me, you have voodoo magic powers that include telepathy, then all this may be less of an issue for you. But if your powers are those of mere mortals, then it's worth staying alert to the hazards of e-mail communication, something John clearly didn't appreciate.

His e-mails were typically lengthy affairs that'd compete easily with a short novel, often cc'd to every being on the planet and, I suspect, bcc'd to aliens on other planets too. He would mix up too many different, unrelated points, jumping from one to another and back, in a convoluted way that left one bewildered. I always had to scratch my head a few times after reading his e-mails.

Unless your goal is to provoke similar head-scratching by your e-mail recipients, it's always better to keep your e-mails clear and concise, sticking to, at most, two or three related points as much as possible, and explaining them in a coherent way.

It's also worth considering the likely emotional re-actions of the recipients, and whether those feelings are what you want to elicit.

And you should remember that an e-mail isn't meant to serve like the drumbeats used by my ancestors for communications, which could be heard by all and sundry, including their domestic animals and those in the forest. It's far better to critically think through who really needs to be aware of the communication and why.

I myself was cognisant of all these points as I crafted the first of my two e-mails. It was addressed to John himself. I copied in Layla, everyone in my team, my immediate peers on Layla's management team and our HR Business Partner. I made sure I expressed my message clearly. I thanked John for his prior work running the department, which I intended to build on, and for his support during the handover period. I also stated explicitly that the man-agement handover was over and, henceforth, all issues and decisions related to the department were entirely my responsibility. I clarified that he would no longer play any part in the departmental affairs, and if anyone within or outside the company brought a related issue to him, perhaps because they were unaware of the management change, he must direct the person to me.

I ended the e-mail by thanking John again. Then I saved it as a "Draft" before printing it.

My second e-mail was addressed to the heads of all PSN stakeholder departments. I copied John in, as well as my team and Layla. I deliberately wrote it in the tone of a formal notification, conveying the same key message – that the handover was officially over and I was now fully responsible for all departmental matters. I included an additional clarification that I would be entrenching robust governance across our product supply operations as a matter of utmost priority, ensuring adherence to company policies and functional procedures, and that I would deal with any non-compliance as a breach and enforce the defined disciplinary actions with HR. I said I was grateful for their anticipated support in boosting *the company's* PSN capability. I ended this e-mail by asking each of the recipients to please cascade my communication to their teams to ensure full awareness.

I knew it was strongly worded. And I knew it would raise a few eyebrows. Most of all, I knew it would grab the attention of one or two miscreants, especially the mention of disciplinary actions. It was my opening salvo to John's few accomplices who were aiding and abetting his subversive efforts.

I saved the second e-mail and printed it also.

Then I re-read and tweaked each one to make sure my message was easily understood, my desired outcomes were clear, my tone reflected my objectives and my spelling and grammar were correct.

A sense of sangfroid seemed to radiate from within me as I locked both e-mail printouts in my desk drawer. I couldn't quite understand it, though I wasn't trying to. It was like the feeling of relief and inner certainty that comes from finding your way after getting lost in a world without a name.

I still thought John's effrontery was astonishing and his actions were reprehensible. But I no longer felt a victim of his crusade.

Sometimes it isn't just about tactics or techniques with stakeholders, but also about mental attitude. Perhaps the composure that was now enveloping me resulted from consciously switching my mentality to assertiveness.

They say a picture says a thousand words. Yet a few words can paint a million pictures, especially when those words are well crafted and targeted. I wanted to be sure that the picture painted by the words in my e-mails reflected my true intent. So I deliberately waited till the next day before sending both e-mails, after reading each one yet again. Haste and regret are habitual bedfellows. And hitting the e-mail "Send" button in a hurry often ends up causing regrettable repercussions.

Regret had no role in my game plan. I would make haste slowly. Henceforth, I'd be dancing to a different drumbeat, and I'd make damn sure John was nowhere near the drums.

# CHAPTER 11

OVER THE NEXT COUPLE OF days, I followed up my e-mails by moving my team back to their original location, after apologising to them for the toing and froing. I also went to see the heads of our stakeholder departments; I spoke to each of them individually, softening the edges of my e-mail while reiterating my key message.

I had already been developing good relationships with most of them, and I'd previously had candid conversations with a couple to get valuable morsels of information on the issues I was dealing with. Many of them could sense what was afoot. I left each one of them in no doubt of my determination and renewed focus.

A critical aspect of that focus was a radical change in how I handled John. I detached myself emotionally, creating a vacuum of sorts between us. I threw away all thoughts of likeability – I couldn't care less anymore whether or not John liked me; trying to foster interpersonal warmth between us had proven to be a lost cause. I became firmer but always assertive in my dealings with him, letting him know unequivocally that I was no pushover and I would not be cowed.

There's often a fine line between assertiveness and aggressiveness, one that is easy to miss and step over. Earlier in my career I'd learned some of the distinguishing mental and behavioural traits of assertiveness. So I was always careful not to adopt an aggressive stance with John. I refrained from thinking and acting in a hostile, abusive or abrasive manner, and tried not to waste unnecessary brainpower or emotional energy on him. I just wouldn't roll in his muck anymore; when you roll with a pig, you both get covered in muck but the pig likes it.

While I acknowledged John's feelings about losing his job to me, I also acknowledged my own rights and needs, and I took a tough stand against his attempted meddling. For instance, he habitually made a big show of highlighting any little operational failure in the PSN department during our fortnightly management team meetings with Layla. Whereas previously I'd try to accept responsibility and downplay the drama without attacking him, now I started to handle his histrionics more robustly. I remember once replying, in an agreeable-yet-firm manner, "Well, you're right, John, that programme is late and it's the PSN department's fault. I'm already looking into this and other similar failures, and it's clear that the root causes of the programme failures stem from the deficient processes within the department – processes which *you* introduced and had been using with the same problems before I took over. None of these programme issues are new."

He shifted uncomfortably in his seat but said nothing.

"Anyway, I'm already working on revamping our departmental processes to eradicate these problems," I continued, as I slowly swept my eyes across my colleagues at the table, keeping my gaze relaxed and confident. "And with the continued support of everyone here and your teams, we will be successful in stamping out these problem issues."

I knew John made these public shows to make me look incapable and score points with Layla. Yet I also knew he was starting to get the message that I was pre-pared to unsheathe my sword if need be.

On a separate occasion, when he tried to amend one of our departmental procedures under the guise of his role as "… the Process and Systems lead for Layla's organisation", I thanked him for his concern but stated forcefully and categorically that I was wholly responsible for the department and our operating procedures, that revamping the whole kit and caboodle was exactly what Layla had appointed me for, and that *I* would specify our working practices and tools, not him. I made sure to do this in writing as well, adding that I'd communicate our new procedures to him at the appropriate time on our transformation journey.

Indeed, I redoubled my efforts to speed up the jour-ney and transform every aspect of the PSN department. Working over the weekends at home was part of the gig. And a tough gig it was too. But as with many things in life, the harder the struggle, the sweeter the victory.

My victory started to show in many ways. My team, which I had invigorated with fresh blood and lots of inspiration, guidance and confidence, grew into the professional, savvy group we really needed to be. Our en-hanced processes were increasingly helping us pre-empt operational problems and yielding more and more programmes on track, as evident on the departmental performance scorecard I had introduced. Our stakeholder departments and key senior executives welcomed these improvements with relief. They became active members of the burgeoning PSN Fan Club, as did Layla and my colleagues in her management team.

These were all welcome changes to the inferno of fires I had inherited. But even more welcome yet shocking was the change in the chief arsonist's attitude and behaviour.

I was amazed that my assertive temperament with John seemed to impact him in ways I couldn't have guessed. The dynamics of our relationship changed completely. He seemed to morph into a different person, certainly in his dealings with me and my team, as if my continued assertiveness neutralised his rancour. He became less of a pain. The meddling eventually stopped. And he seemed to respect me more.

Our relationship didn't quite have the degree of sweetness I tend to prefer, but the increased absence of animosity suited me well. I accepted that John may just not have been the type for chummy bonhomie with me. I knew that stakeholders' personalities differ, some more agreeable than others, just as with people in general. For example, some people dislike friendliness and chewing the fat – they prefer you to get straight to the point, in a logical and impersonal manner; some dislike directness and abruptness – they prefer to bond or connect on a personal level with lots of warmth and camaraderie; some people find structure, process and routine quite inhibiting – they'd rather explore ideas and analyse options with resourcefulness and ingenuity; and some dislike theories, hypotheses and intuitive assertions – they prefer hard, concrete facts which are specific and verifiable. The more you can calibrate your style to an individual stakeholder's quirks and dispositions, the easier it'll be to achieve what you want with them, through them or from them.

What I'd wanted was to deliver what Layla had tasked me with.

Which I did.

The successful turnaround of the PSN department is one of the highlights of my corporate career. It felt that way at the time, and I imagine I'll always look back on it that way.

Yet the turnaround in my relationship with John was just as momentous. All these years later, I'm still somewhat baffled by it. It certainly reinforced my belief that, as desirable as it may be, it's not *always* possible to have harmonious, pleasant interactions with *all* stakeholders; some situations require the degree of firmness intrinsic to assertiveness.

It also taught me that the human spirit has unparalleled strength and fortitude within it. Even in the face of untold suffering and seemingly insurmountable barriers, we have something inside us that is so strong and wise, something resilient that is always there for us to tap into, a force or power that resides within *every one* of us and can help us overcome the toughest challenges, whether it's a formidably difficult stakeholder or some other devastating impediment. But to harness this inborn power, we've got to devote time and attention to "looking inside", where the power resides, rather than becoming fixated with the outside world, where the challenge originates. Looking outside, at the world around you, can teach you a lot. Yet looking inside, at the world inside you, can teach you even more.

My experience with Dickhead John helped impart this intelligence to me.

It also showed me that Dickhead John wasn't really a dickhead – he was just caught up in the throes of intense negative vibes at losing his job to me, perhaps a victim of his primal emotions.

I too could fall prey to my primal inclinations and hold a grudge against him, because he brought me so much suffering. But growth often feels like suffering. So instead, I thank him for contributing to my career growth. And I send him voodoo love, because love is the sweetest of all primal emotions.

# THE FLAME OF
# STAKEHOLDER LOVE

# CHAPTER 12

I GUESS LOVE WASN'T THE emotion Amandine was feeling as she responded, "But they should just do as they're told!"

The look of indignation and bafflement on her face told me so.

I'd had a suspicion that she might react as such. I had grown accustomed to this sort of reaction from my work helping people grow their workplace effectiveness. But I'd first recognised it in my own self many years earlier. It was a reaction I'd learned to deal with, one that often accompanied my efforts to convey both positive and difficult messages constructively.

In truth, my message to Amandine wasn't really "difficult" per se. It was just hard to comprehend for the organisationally naïve, as I myself had been all those years ago.

As an intern, there was no way Amandine Fournier would have been exposed to the intricacies of managing workplace stakeholders with aplomb, such that things just fall into place like a well-choreographed ballet. She was still in the final stages of her MSc studies, which she'd pretty much started straight after her first degree. With little or no professional work experience, she'd innocently swallowed her academic tutelage hook, line and sinker – she obviously expected that the way things work in organisations is the way the textbooks describe.

But we can only ever truly learn about some things by doing them or experiencing them. It's easy to talk about surviving in the jungle when you've never actually experienced that necessity. The Faculty of Hard Knocks at the University of Life was established to give us hands-on learning about jungle survival.

I know this first-hand from my own follies in the organisational jungle.

And I reckon you do too.

Amandine was finding this out bit by bit.

I knew she was having to recalibrate her expectations, something that isn't always easy for some of us. Yet managing expectations is such an important element of workplace effectiveness and success.

Unrealistic expectations can wreak havoc on your job performance and work life, and are perilous to your stakeholder management efforts. Calibrating expectations helps us reframe the way we see the world, hence bringing greater harmony to our work.

This isn't just about our own expectations, but also those of our stakeholders. Failing to properly manage stakeholders' expectations causes dissatisfaction, and can make people become unaccommodating, combative or intransigent.

Whereas when you pay adequate attention to their opinions and expectations, and ensure appropriate calibration of those expectations to secure mutual alignment, you're engendering a greater chance for smoother engagements with your stakeholders and a higher likelihood of your work success.

In doing this, it may be necessary to drill down and clarify the hopes, assumptions and reasoning that underpin stakeholders' expectations. Subsequently, you should provide assurance on those that are valid or acceptable, and bring stakeholders down to earth on those under-pinnings that are pure fantasy – in a considerate manner.

It's important to provide clarity and common understanding of the goals, direction, scope, deliverables, timescales and risks of the relevant work activity or initiative, and ensure the vision of what is desired or "what success looks like" is widely communicated, along with clearly defined and sensible measures of success. Depending on the task, project or initiative and the context, it may even be advisable to go as far as specifying or jointly agreeing precise ways of working, such as the frequency and means of communication.

And it may be just as wise to define to stakeholders, or agree with them, what aspects of the work are "must-haves", "nice-to-haves" and "won't-haves". It helps reduce ambiguity and the scope for misunderstandings.

It sounds a bit patronising to say that all this should be done up front, as early as possible, and also re-visited as appropriate on an ongoing basis. Yet I've witnessed many stakeholder hostilities and skirmishes that stemmed from such oversight.

And many, too, caused by a simple failure to deliver what was promised.

Unfulfilled promises and expectations can be hurtful to the human spirit and leave a bitter aftertaste in the psyche. Maybe that's why some people prefer not to have great expectations of success at work or in their careers – perhaps it's a way of sheltering themselves from the storms and vagaries of life, so their hearts don't suffer the unwelcome taste of bitterness and discontent if things don't work out as they expected or dreamed. But such folks forget that you can't have a dream come true if you have no dream in the first place, as Oscar Hammerstein II reminds us in *South Pacific*.

Having some expectations – even if only to wake up tomorrow – is part of the human drama. Calibrating our expectations, difficult as it may sometimes be, may, perhaps, be a safe and healthy way to keep us in tune with the realities of life, the same realities Amandine was discovering. Her initial expectations about organisational life were a bit idealistic.

My own expectations were more modest.

I certainly didn't expect Amandine to have grasped the nitty-gritty of effective stakeholder management. I didn't expect her to know, for example, that when we engage stakeholders, we should have in our minds if not our hands remedies to a critical question they may be pondering: "What's in it for me?"; that our remedies and propositions must show that we're working in stakeholders' interests, to help *them* win at their game legitimately; and that, although it may not always seem like it, our stakeholders are mostly working for the same outcome as us: ultimately, the success of the organisation. And I didn't expect her to already know that, in some ways, winning over stakeholders is a bit like winning over or seducing a love interest; but it's a seduction without flowers, chocolates or love songs.

Although she wasn't laughing just now, Amandine had burst into a hearty and infectious laugh the first time I'd told her that.

I went on to explain that when one is wooing a potential love interest, we tend to only see their good points. And the predominant themes in our thoughts and actions are getting to know them better, and convincing them of all the joy and sweetness that awaits – if they'd just hook up with us. The flowers and chocolates are like the early signs we use to indicate the proposition on offer. And we continue to invest considerable time and effort to turn the potential or nascent liaison into romance.

It's somewhat the same with stakeholders at work. Although we may not always see their good points immediately – we may have to continuously make the effort to look for the good in each person or each stakeholder situation, which isn't always easy, especially if your stakeholder is being insufferable. Still, *we do* want to get our groove on with our stakeholders. That's what effective stakeholder management is about. If we're going to hook up with them successfully, we have to invest time and energy in convincing them that their engagement with us will yield bountiful sweetness – for them and their work.

But instead of flowers or love songs, we have to woo stakeholders with our wisdom, the wisdom that emanates from recognising that the word "stakeholder" inherently enshrines a fundamental tenet: stakeholders are important because they have some skin in our game – they have a stake in the work we do. In which case, doesn't it make sense to really get a fix on these folks and their worlds, including their work operations, their problems and the issues that frustrate them? Doesn't it make sense to pause from our busyness as frequently as possible and view ourselves, our work and our operating style from the outside, so we can perceive what our stakeholders see, and shape or tweak our game accordingly?

We harness our wisdom by adopting a seduction game plan that demonstrates the benefits stakeholders will enjoy by hooking up with us.

How we go about our seduction will vary from situation to situation. For example, the way we handle individual stakeholders may differ from how we handle stakeholders as groups. Likewise, the most effective approach for dealing with frontline stakeholders may differ from how we deal with middle managers. And the mechanisms and tactics that prove fruitful when engaging with a bunch of techie geeks in the IT or engineering functions may not necessarily have the same impact with a bunch of creatives in marketing.

Quite simply, despite what many "experts" out there say or imply, there is no single universal panacea to the challenge of managing stakeholders with flair. But there are many effective principles and approaches we can adopt – like those I learned from Ralph Patrick and from my enforced pilgrimage instigated by John Reed, and those I used at Ribbexo.

How in the world could I possibly expect a greenhorn intern like Amandine to already know all this!

She would eventually, as her professional career evolved. But right now it was incumbent on me to explain things to her and help her get the hang of organisational realities. Which is exactly what I'd been doing since she joined my team.

*

At the time, I was responsible for Global Operations at Ostara Industries, a large industrial manufacturing and services business headquartered in Switzerland. I had been appointed onto the group leadership team with the primary aim of creating a seamless functional infrastructure, by consolidating and optimising our operations in twelve countries across the Americas, Europe, Middle East, Africa and Asia-Pacific.

From my prior experience of establishing or harmonising global functions, I had known it would be a demanding task. When I'd led similar initiatives previously, I had ended up spending more time in planes and airports than in my office. It had sort of felt like propagating a new religion; a prophet can't disseminate and embed new beliefs and ways of worship without mingling with his people.

In these situations, people in the local operations – this time, in countries as far-flung as Canada, Chile and China – are used to doing their own thing. They often dislike or resent what they see as interference from head office, especially when it requires changes to their established ways of working, their personnel or their operating model.

As I expected, the distaste or discomfort wasn't just felt by employees and executives one would view as "stakeholders" in the conventional sense. My own in-country managers and functional teams in the regional businesses needed much reassurance and hand-holding through the change, and I saw them, too, as my stakeholders.

I understood the resentment. And I appreciated how unsettling such transformative change can be. So rather than bulldozing my way through, I was investing substantial effort in making the transformation journey as easy as possible for everyone affected.

It was time-consuming. And I was yet again shuttling between different company locations worldwide. It seemed almost pointless having a beautiful, high-rise office just off the shores of Lake Geneva, with scenic views across much of the cheerful, bustling city centre, the breathtaking backdrop of the mountains and the majestic fountain on the lake, Jet d'Eau, just a short walk away. The panoramic views from my office window offered a splendid vista that always brought a happy smile to my face. Yet my travels prevented me from revelling in that splendour to my heart's content.

But I didn't begrudge shuttling around the world like the United Nations Secretary-General. My globetrotting was driven by my belief that it's vitally important to *proactively make time* for stakeholder relationships.

Rather than viewing stakeholder relationship management as an add-on to the job, something that detracts from your "real" job, or something that only needs attention when things are not smooth, it should be an integral part of your modus operandi – even if you're not managing a change programme.

Whatever your job role is, devoting a proportion of your day or week – say, ten, fifteen, twenty percent of your time, or whatever feels right – to relationship-building will be one of the best investments you'll make in your career growth.

This is so valuable that I've gone as far as specifying it as part of job descriptions on some occasions.

Even if it isn't explicitly stated in your formal job specification, and even when you have nothing concrete to discuss with your stakeholders, spending time pressing the flesh is still a worthwhile endeavour, not least because it helps build trust and social capital, thus oiling the wheels for your success and helping you grow your likeability.

I had been counselling Amandine on such stakeholder management principles and approaches in another of our regular one-on-one chats when she made her indignant retort. She obviously expected that as the top dog I should just bark out my orders, and people would "… just do as they're told".

It wasn't the first time her comments revealed her inexperience. But I was patient with her, just as I had to be with other stakeholders. Because patience is one of the magic ingredients for conjuring success in any endeavour. A patient person will always eat ripe fruit, as the African proverb says.

You too may need to be patient with some of your stakeholders, so the fruits of your effort can ripen for your eventual benefit. To paraphrase St. Augustine, your patience is the companion of your wisdom, the very same wisdom at the crux of your seduction effort.

# CHAPTER 13

My patience with Amandine never wore thin. And I never wearied of giving her my time, despite the demands of the transformation I was driving.

It wasn't the ideal circumstance to take on board an intern who I'd known would need lots of guidance and encouragement to gain real value from the experience. That's why I had initially been reluctant to bring her into my team.

But her enthusiasm, intelligence and personality had swung the decision. I liked her attitude. Even her organisational naivety brought an indescribable air of innocence, novelty and honesty that was quite refreshing.

I sensed that she'd go far in her career. And I remembered how valuable my own undergraduate internship had been for my career. Besides, I knew I could carve out bite-sized projects for her that would stretch her a bit, teach her a lot and help her grow – as long as I complemented that with giving her good support.

I had tasked her with developing a common group-wide process for Supplier Performance Management, to replace the asinine, disjointed or non-existent activities we had in different countries. It was one of the deliverables on my transformation plan, although it wasn't an immediate priority; her work would dovetail into the wider change programme further down the line.

In effect, what she was doing was saving me some future work and preparing an important piece of the jigsaw to be slotted into place at the appropriate time. So I had every reason to want her to succeed, aside from the good I knew it would do her mojo.

She was collaborating with colleagues in our businesses across the globe. And I was doing my bit to clear the way for her behind the scenes.

Understandably, she was coming up against some of the apathetic and uncooperative attitudes we sometimes find in stakeholders. I was steering her through the minefield of stakeholder engagement, trying to infuse the benefit of my experience into her approach, while simultaneously fostering her own initiative by encouraging her to take the bull by the horns.

When you lead people, whether in a project team or functional organisation, there's often a temptation to just tell them what to do and how to do it. This doesn't help them grow, as it doesn't stretch them.

As a leader, if all you want is for people to do the work without learning a lot from doing it, then simply command them. But if you want your people to grasp and learn from the nuances or intricacies of the work they do, and how it relates to your functional or project goals and those of the wider organisation, then take the time to break it down and explore it with them, giving appropriate guidance and motivation. It really is the old "catching fish for people versus teaching them to catch fish" thing. You can direct people to achieve results, or you can focus on helping them learn to direct themselves effectively.

In truth, it's more than a leadership thing that pertains solely to managing people who report to us in project or functional teams. To some degree, it also applies to how we "manage" stakeholders. The more information you share with a stakeholder about the work you're doing, or trying to do, *in collaboration with them*, and the more relevant that information is, the more likely they are to gain deeper, better and more valuable insights – into your agenda and how meaningful it is to their own work activities and organisational existence. Making stakeholders feel that you and your work bring value and sweetness beyond chocolates, flowers and love songs is a fabulous way to avoid or reduce organisational resistance.

Of course, to sell and deliver that value, you have to find the right levers to exploit. Flowers, chocolates and the accoutrements of love will be inadequate to secure the gate pass to where you really want to be with your stakeholders.

You may also have to learn to persevere.

When your stakeholder management efforts are not producing the results you want, clearly you must review your modus operandi to see what alterations you need to make. These could be any number of things. For example, you may need to be more forthcoming with acknowledging concessions from stakeholders or positive changes they've made; or be more earnest about the things that aren't working despite all efforts, and perhaps suggest that you both escalate the issues to someone higher up, in a joint effort to seek progress; or be direct and ask the stakeholder to help you understand what could be done to change the game positively; or you may need to overcome your avoidance of conflict, and master how to handle it professionally; or you may need to learn to choose your proverbial battles wisely – some are not worth the energy, and some turn out to be wasteful confrontations with stakeholders who really have no ultimate authority on the issue of contention nor the influence or power to impact your destiny.

But sometimes your stakeholder management efforts need no adjustments and it's simply a case of staying persistent.

In such situations, it is worth remembering that your stakeholders are really no different from the general population in a sense – they are people, not farm animals or pets in training; and people don't always embrace change right away or welcome new ideas and learning with open arms. That includes me, you and Amandine.

*

I knew my perseverance with Amandine would pay off handsomely in expanding her organisational enlightenment. Despite her occasional ingenuous responses and comments, I could tell her development gap was already narrowing. The alignment between her perspective and organisational reality was growing – at the pace that these things take.

I continued with my efforts, giving her advice, probing her thinking, feelings and observations, playing devil's advocate, using role-play to help her practise her communication and interaction approaches, and sharing details of my own approaches and experiences at Ostara, as well as learning points from prior stakeholder management escapades.

I told her about my experience with John Reed years earlier, and how his malevolence had almost wrecked my sanity. Yet he wasn't the only challenge I'd had to contend with in transforming the PSN operations at Tempura Products. As was now happening again at Ostara, the team I'd inherited back then needed almost as much attention as stakeholders in other functions. It was imperative to hold a shared perspective of what we were doing and where we were headed with my own team; our unity and collective view was a prerequisite for the transformation to be successful.

Selling my transformation agenda to my PSN team remains one of my most memorable examples of leveraging the power of images and analogies.

Sometimes, in winning people over and keeping them supportive of your agenda, it's best to articulate your intent or sell your vision with imagery. After all, a picture can indeed say a thousand words. But to be effective in achieving the desired result, the vision must be clear and compelling enough to inspire people into a unified mass of focused endeavour, and communicated in a way that gets their juices flowing.

Enthusing my team and galvanising them into cohesive teamwork was definitely needed in the chaotic PSN world I'd inherited.

The PSN department's responsibility for defining production and distribution networks for all Tempura's products necessitated day-to-day liaisons with key stakeholder departments like Marketing, Engineering, Logistics, Finance and Manufacturing. And they were all at war.

The Marketing guys made commitments to customers before products or upgrades were available for market supply, and sometimes before Engineering had even designed them. Engineering felt that Manufacturing was too slow and unwieldy, and hindered their product development roadmaps. Manufacturing was constantly irked by Marketing's dodgy sales forecasts; most Manufacturing people thought the Marketing guys were smarmy jerks and that the product engineers lived in cloud cuckoo land. The Logistics guys just wanted to be left alone to play with their forklifts and pallets. And Finance … well, I think they just saw everything and everyone as dollar signs in their endless spreadsheets; and when those dollars didn't add up to big fat profit margins, Finance became a pain to everyone. In the middle of all this anarchy, caught between the warring stakeholder functions and their stray bullets, was the PSN department, which ended up fighting everyone else.

Honestly, "chaotic" isn't an exaggeration of the situation I inherited.

It was very much like the Wild West.

To ensure my team grasped the essence of the transformation we were about to undertake, I clarified to them that the new PSN department we had to mutate into was every bit like the group of cowboys in the old American western TV series *Rawhide*; while everybody working in PSN operations was running berserk like crazed cattle, we – the transformed PSN department – would "round 'em up" and marshal the PSN activities into an orderly, coherent and reliable programme of structured projects, bringing sanity and stability to the current chaos.

I had created a two-image illustration to bring the *Rawhide* analogy to life. The first image depicted a scene of mayhem, in which countless cattle ran amok in a prairie, while a handful of cowboys sat astride their horses forlornly, looking overwhelmed and impotent amidst the melee. And the second image showed the mounted cowboys, complete with lassos, looking self-assured and in control, having corralled the animals into a disciplined herd, moving along on their cattle drive in an orderly manner, towards a bullseye target in the near distance.

I thought it was a fitting illustration to accompany the *Rawhide* analogy. And in the first couple of months or so, I always used it at the start and end of my weekly team meetings – because consistency and repetition are key to successfully positioning a message in people's psyches.

This is something that can be easily forgotten in our interactions and communications with stakeholders.

Consistency and repetition of your message helps nail the point home with your stakeholders. When things are repeated consistently, they're more likely to break through and seep into our deeper consciousness.

And once embedded, quite often, before we know it they start influencing, if not controlling, our perspectives, our thinking and our actions.

It's a bit like hearing a catchy jingle or a song repeatedly, and even if you don't quite like the song, before you know it, it's repeating in your mind over and over again, or you find yourself whistling the jingle or humming the tune time and time again. And it's a bit like how we learned many things in our first years at school, like multiplication – "2 x 2 = 4", "2 x 2 = 4", "2 x 2 = 4" …; see it or hear it consistently often enough and it soon sticks. Just like the earworm jingle or song.

When you're consistent and repetitive with a compelling and well-crafted message, the chances of getting your gist to stick in the minds of your stakeholders increase significantly.

I didn't just want my *Rawhide* message to stick in the minds of my departmental family members – the nucleus of my stakeholder groups – I wanted it to be the ethos of our organisational existence in those first few months.

My team members exploded into hilarious laughter the first time I used the *Rawhide* presentation slides to illustrate our transformation intent. I have a feeling they probably thought I was a bit mad.

And yet they got it.

They also grasped our part in the mayhem.

When the laughter had died down, it was clear that they not only understood the message, but were also very attracted and inspired by the vision of a calmer, more organised and systematic working environment.

It wasn't long before they themselves were using the *Rawhide* analogy in conversations with me, and, I suspect, with their stakeholders. Some of them even asked me to e-mail them the *Rawhide* illustration.

I continued to use the analogy in our team meetings and one-on-one chats with my staff, and I sometimes alluded to it in my discussions with my stakeholder peers and their teams.

My discussions with our stakeholder departments reflected several themes. But a core element was selling the transformation vision. I was making sure my stakeholders could comprehend and buy into it well enough, such that it became a shared intent; I knew that they too were frustrated by the disarray and myriad problems of our communal PSN world. The appeal and motivation of a more disciplined way of working, which would make *their* lives easier, allowed me to hook into their desire and enlist their commitment as partners in the transformation initiative. I wasn't "doing the change" *to* them, rather I was doing it *with* them.

Just like my PSN team way back then, Amandine found the *Rawhide* analogy amusing. I had actually dug up the presentation slides from some old files on my laptop to show her the illustration as I recounted the story.

She was still chuckling as she asked, "But weren't they offended? I mean …, to be portrayed as crazed cattle running around wildly – didn't that annoy them?"

It was a brilliant question.

It led me to spell out to her the importance of communicating with finesse.

There's so much more to this than mere words. Sometimes we say the right things in the wrong way or the wrong things in the right way. Communicating the right things in the right way is often the critical factor in ensuring our message is well received, and is so cogent as to induce the end results we desire.

Spicing your stakeholder communications with finesse isn't always easy. I know from my own personal experience of making some real gaffes earlier in my career. Yet I also know that one can always improve – by continually practising and making necessary refinements.

And I know, too, that if you look around you and identify colleagues who are effective operators – those who are adept at influencing others without coercion – you'll notice that they typically communicate with an abundance of finesse. They draw on insights into human psychology which signify universal principles, many of which I'm sharing with you now, just as I shared them with Amandine.

I may not be an effective operator with everyone every time. But I was with most of my PSN stakeholders back then.

I had to be careful that I didn't give the impression that *they* were the problem – running around like the crazed cattle. Rather, I put the spotlight on our collective disarray, and the problems and frustrations we were all suffering, making sure I got my message across in a constructive way. This wasn't about slamming or fighting them; I accepted their spheres of responsibility and authority, which made them as much architects of the disarray as victims of it.

Sometimes, when we're leading change that is hugely problematic, or when the situation with stakeholders is quite horrendous, we can unwittingly end up developing negative sentiments about our stakeholders, or some of them, to such an extent that we begin to demonise them or taint them as the "enemy" in our psyche. It's a serious handicap that can detract from your seduction efforts. If you find yourself in that situation, it's helpful to remind yourself that your perspective or attitude may be the real enemy, not your stakeholders.

I tried to remember this, despite the unique challenges created by one particular stakeholder: the one-time arsonist, Dickhead John.

# CHAPTER 14

THE PROBLEMS JOHN GAVE ME were mostly distinctive from the generic issues I faced with other stakeholders. In channelling my seduction efforts at winning these stakeholders over and keeping them onside, I was also amassing social pressure to isolate John and his arson antics – the more I succeeded with the wider community of PSN stakeholders, the more it made John conspicuous as an antagonist. Even he must have picked up on that. And I suppose it was a contributory factor in his subsequent metamorphosis, helping to alter the dynamic between us eventually. All the while, I remained focused on stimulating and fostering positive vibes with my broader stakeholder community.

I had to keep thinking like a good salesman, never losing sight of the importance of convincing my stakeholders of the benefits I proffered, while making sure I indeed delivered on my seduction promise as the PSN transformation progressed.

The idea of thinking like a salesperson might trigger an instinctive mental recoil in some of us. Maybe because it immediately sounds distasteful or unappealing. It probably conjures up images of a snake-oil salesman with low ethical standards. Yet, if you think about it deeply, much of our work entails some form of "selling", not least every instance of asking stakeholders to consider or accept a different perspective or a new angle on things.

We may not have to work hard at selling the perspective, or new angle, or different way of working or interacting. But the very fact that it's new or different means that, more often than not, there's inherently some element of "sales" involved in stakeholders "buying" into and accepting our proposition.

The notion of an inherent element of sales in our work is something you may have to recognise and embrace to be successful in the workplace, especially if your definition of success includes climbing up the career ladder; because we're selling almost all the time, knowingly or unknowingly – selling ourselves, our personal brand, ideas, visions, new practices, and so on, to our staff, our bosses, our peers and our stakeholders.

In fact, life itself entails lots of selling and buying. For example, right from childhood our parents sell us a rubric of morality and, generally speaking, we buy into it; we sell our best selves to love interests, who buy into the potential happiness and sweetness we convey and end up as our spouses and lovers; prophets, gurus and all manner of religions sell us doctrines and beliefs which we buy into; even your boss or employer sold you a career opportunity which you bought into and led you to the very job you're doing now.

Clearly, thinking and acting like a good salesperson with our stakeholders doesn't have to mean we're sleazy snake-oil salespeople; not if we remain in tune with our moral compass.

I was quite pleased that it didn't take Amandine long to warm to this concept. I suspect it had as much to do with my elucidation as her own developing understanding, fuelled by her ongoing direct experience.

As she told me herself in one of our chats, trying to form the habit of thinking like a saleswoman with her stakeholders forced her to consider up front what they might be thinking or feeling. We both agreed that some might be worried about stability or job security, fearing that her project would significantly change the nature and content of their work or make their job redundant. Some might be feeling overworked and resentful about giving up their time to engage with her – especially if they deemed her work to be less important than their existing workload, unlikely to be beneficial to them personally or just another organisational pipe dream. And some might be worried that her enquiries and analyses would show up the scant grasp they had of their work or how meagre their organisational contribution really was.

She said such pre-considerations helped her anticipate, or at least try to, how her stakeholders might react prior to any specific engagement or discussion.

Hearing this kind of feedback from Amandine was testament to her emerging wings, and it brought the joys of spring to my soul. There are few things more rewarding than helping another human spirit to flourish.

In time, she'd be spreading those wings to fly.

Her budding awareness and acumen reinforced my confidence in her. And I continued to regale her with various nuggets of learning I'd picked up or consolidated, in tandem with jointly reviewing and analysing her own stakeholder engagements.

We explored the differences and commonalities between the seduction stuff we do with stakeholders up front and the stuff we continue to do on an ongoing basis – just like we do some stuff up front to win a love interest's heart initially, and then, to keep them happy and their hearts filled with love, we continue to do other stuff recurrently, like surprising them with romantic dates, giving them our full attention, lavishing them with endearments, doing various tasks for them, and listening to their hopes and dreams.

It's easy to overlook these differences and common-alities – in our relationships with lovers and spouses and in our relationships with stakeholders. Sometimes we're successful with our initial seduction efforts with stake-holders, and then we become complacent or negligent and things may start to turn sour or lose a bit of sweet-ness. In these situations, it's almost as if we start to take our stakeholders and the mutual benefits we share with them for granted, albeit unintentionally.

Communication is one of those activities that span both the "up front" and the "ongoing" domains. It's of the utmost importance to maintain constant communication with your stakeholders, even when things feel like *la dolce vita*. Communicating constantly with stakeholders is so vital – especially in change management situations – that some folks say you can't overcommunicate.

Certainly, it's true that when communication ceases or lulls, a vacuum occurs, and that vacuum can easily become filled with hearsay, misinformation or propaganda. That's one of the reasons you'll find that any change management plan worth its salt will include "Communication" as a critical work stream.

You too should incorporate communication as a critical element of your work with stakeholders – even if you can't always quite find the spice jar labelled "Finesse".

And in doing so, it's worth distinguishing between the possible differing needs of your different stakeholders or stakeholder groups. Just as your engagement tactics with the IT techie geeks may need to be different from your tactics with the marketing creatives or the finance bean counters, your communications game plan may need to be adaptable to cover the unique or special interests of your multiple stakeholder entities.

If you don't make the effort to communicate robustly, providing regular follow-ups, feedback and updates, and continuing to take your ears to every stakeholder interaction, you're not sustaining awareness and exchange. And you risk alienating your stakeholder community. In effect, you're doing yourself a disservice.

My follies and victories over the years have taught me that one of the best ways of instilling a more fruitful take on stakeholder communications is to tweak our insights and perspectives on stakeholders, by starting to see them as "customers", "consumers" or "investors". After all, since they have a stake in our game, that kind of makes them investors in our work. And since they get *something* from our efforts, then they're just like a consumer or customer of our work output.

When we talk about "customers", most of us automatically think of the external customer who buys or receives our organisation's products or services. Indeed, my own first foray into the concept of "stakeholders as customers" was when I was running a manufacturing unit early in my career; I was instituting a culture of quality, where every single individual was responsible for assuring our product quality to customers. It required everyone to adopt the philosophy of doing things "right first time", rather than relying on the Quality Control section to spot product defects. It was a radical departure from the erstwhile "numbers culture", where the priority was just to hit the production output targets, despite the unacceptably high levels of scrap, reworks and customer returns.

I spent the vast majority of my time on the shop floor, interacting with my production operators and supervisors, observing attitudes and behaviours right where people got their hands dirty in the daily grind, giving constant encouragement and feedback, and unceasingly preaching about the end-customers who would eventually receive the batches of products being manufactured there and then.

As well as my impromptu shop-floor sermons, at my weekly team meetings I routinely spelled out the importance of our customers as prime stakeholders in our manufacturing operations. They must have a hundred percent faith in our product quality, rather than the disruptions and pain we were currently causing them.

I clarified to my people the impacts of the customer experience on our company's reputation as a supplier and its long-term fortunes. And I stressed the consequences this could have on our own jobs. Every one of us had to keep the end-customer at the forefront of our minds in everything we did day in, day out – happy and satisfied customers would yield long-term job prosperity.

There's no doubt that the Total Quality Management (TQM) training the company put us through was a significant contributor to the twenty-four percent reduction in customer returns we achieved. It definitely revived something I'd initially been taught in my Manufacturing Systems Engineering degree course: the notion of an "internal customer" – a production process or department within an organisation that receives materials, products or services from a preceding process or department. If the external customer is to be satisfied, then every worker, process or department within the organisation must ensure they satisfy their immediate internal customer.

It's basically the underlying rationale of "stakeholders as customers".

Our stakeholders may not always receive tangible materials or products from us in a manufacturing sense. But the fact that they receive information, service or some form of output, consequence or *impact* from our work means that they are, in effect, our internal customers.

"That's so true, Sigi. It really makes sense," Amandine exclaimed, as she jotted something down in her notebook.

She had been listening to me attentively. And yet again, I sensed that my continued elucidations were washing away the dust of her everyday stakeholder challenges.

I nodded in silent agreement before adding, "Embracing the principle of 'stakeholders as customers' is a little adjustment in thinking and attitude, a nifty mind trick, which helps enhance our personal effectiveness in our stakeholder dealings."

Thinking of stakeholders as customers can have a remarkable effect on your mindset. I'm certain this effect enveloped Amandine's mind momentarily when I asked her, "If you were running your own business and your stakeholders were your customers, how would you handle them, knowing they are the source of your daily bread?"

Most of us would probably handle them more resourcefully, staying focused on satisfying or exceeding their needs. And some of us would be so good at giving them a delightful experience as to make them go "Wow!"

We can apply the same customer-centric ethos, and make great strides in building stakeholder harmony, by incorporating some principles of Customer Relationship Management (CRM) into our approach with stakeholders.

Proactively making time for relationship-building is one of the key aspects of CRM, as I said to Amandine.

I told her about embedding CRM tenets in my regional teams at Ostara, as part of my ongoing shake-up of the Global Operations function. For example, I continuously encouraged my regional managers to routinely go out and spend time with their internal customers each week, just as I myself was doing.

Although some of them had initially resented the "extra work", as they saw it, what with the myriad tasks they already had to address daily, they soon got to appreciate the value. They regularly gave me feedback about how these interactions were proving priceless in discovering golden nuggets of wisdom about their stakeholders and their departments, as well as providing additional opportunities to communicate Global Operations news and updates.

When you try this out yourself, you'll discover that although such interactions don't always have to be formal meetings, they always provide superb avenues to implant your value proposition in your stakeholders' consciousness and operations.

# CHAPTER 15

I HAVE TO ADMIT THAT at first Amandine didn't quite catch on to the notion of imbibing CRM principles in her work. It seemed to me that she understood it at an intellectual level, but couldn't quite fully coalesce it into her day-to-day perspectives and actions.

To me, that was just part of the process of her growth. I myself hadn't always been able to imbibe CRM tenets in my stakeholder activities, and I had many rueful memories of several missteps with stakeholders in my career. I didn't let them disconcert me. They were just footprints in the sands of time. If you're leaving footprints behind you, then you must be moving forward, making progress on establishing your destiny, one footstep after another; you just have to pay attention to your direction of travel.

So I saw my task as helping Amandine identify and navigate the most effective and efficient travel path for her growth and success.

Just as I had done with my managers and regional teams, I expounded to her how we can all learn a great deal from the marketing efforts of successful consumer brands. The most successful consumer product companies target significant efforts at developing a deep understanding of their markets and their customers. They exploit this insight to shape and sustain positive perceptions of their brands and create enduring customer loyalty.

To earn the loyalty of our stakeholders and maximise their faith in us, we too must develop similar deep organisational insights and create a strong brand positioning for ourselves and our work.

As I explained to Amandine, I had done this as part of the transformation of the PSN operations at Tempura Products. And I had done it in several other organisational change initiatives I'd led in my career. Chatting about it woke up memories of one particular instance, many years earlier, where I was leading the turnaround of a Supply Chain Planning and Control department. It was in a medium-sized business that supplied spare parts for maintenance and repair operations in the rail industry. The departmental situation I had come into was almost as dreadful as waking up in a lion's den. Everyone in the team was extremely busy, "working hard" trying to do their jobs as best they could, as they ran helter-skelter from one catastrophe to another. Yet, despite their hard work, the performance was atrocious, the department had an appalling reputation within the company and the relationship with the internal customer was dire.

You don't really need a PhD in organisational psychology to appreciate that entrenching customer-centricity in such a situation was a paramount need. It was one of the cornerstones of my turnaround initiative. And as part of my approach, I relocated my whole department to sit within the internal customer area, after I had discussed the idea with my boss and my opposite number who headed the internal customer department.

The move was a resounding success. It helped to break down barriers and precipitate closer, cooperative working relationships between our departments and between individuals in both teams, which made it easier to remedy the performance deficit.

I was indulging myself a little bit when I told Amandine, "Looking back at it now, I think that co-locating my team with our internal customer was a sublime seduction move. Nothing tells a love interest you mean business like pitching your tent right next to theirs."

She rolled her eyes upwards as she shook her head, laughing softly in amusement. She was obviously happy to allow me my indulgence in attempted witticism.

Being co-located with our internal customer made it easy for our "stakeholder love" to blossom. But, of course, the love was nourished by several other strands of the turnaround, not least instilling a collective CRM mindset among my people – the same thing I was now doing with my Global Operations organisation at Ostara.

Spending time with our internal customers was a brilliant way of cementing the relationship bonds with our key stakeholders; whether it was me doing it at group level with relevant senior executive peers or my Global Operations managers doing it within their regions, it helped grow our brand equity as a function.

The *pièce de résistance* for my regional managers – as they eventually came to discover – was that it also did wonders for their personal brands as individuals.

When your personal brand is shining as bright as the beautiful Mediterranean sun, it feels like your spirit is brimming full of rapture, as it glides effortlessly in a rhapsody of all that is good in life. It's a feeling so blissful, so beyond words and, to borrow a phrase from Charles Handy, quite like a Turkish bath for the soul.

Yet, as I kept reminding my managers, and also mentioned to Amandine, it's always possible to drown in the bath – if you let the sun go to your head and you start thinking you're flawlessly and supremely superfly; you can lose your sense of who you truly are and become a vainglorious nitwit.

This insidious risk manifests when our ego grows unhealthily larger than our gratitude, and jumps in the bath and submerges our spirit in self-conceit.

Just because stakeholders love our groove.

Our ego forgets that stakeholder love has many parallels with romantic love. When you give love, you get it back in return – somehow, somewhere, sometime. And if you keep giving, you'll keep receiving. So, just like Giacomo Casanova, Mata Hari, Cleopatra and all the great seducers in history, we must remember to *continue* to keep our sweethearts filled with love, by enchanting them with delightful and compelling experiences.

One of the most compelling things you can do to secure stakeholder love and keep the flame of love burning bright is to help your stakeholders expand their frame of reference. People generally tend to appreciate others providing experiences and information that enrich their awareness. And a great way to do that with your stakeholders is to share benchmarking information.

Benchmarking information – whether it's internal or external benchmarking – is an invaluable source of intelligence that can provide multiple benefits. Primarily, the intel is always useful to help strengthen or support your argument per se. And it can be uniquely instrumental in orchestrating your romance with aggressive stakeholders in particular. Yet I've also found that stakeholders in general are more willing to be amenable to your requirements or point of view when presented with such objective evidence, especially if the evidence isn't rammed down their throats but presented in a facilitative manner.

It gladdened my heart to hear Amandine's enthusiastic reaction when I suggested that she include benchmarking intel in her discussions with stakeholders. It was very appropriate for her project; for many years, there had been tonnes of information available on the extensive benefits organisations gain from good Supplier Performance

Management, yet a lot of stakeholders in many businesses still don't see it as a priority – until things go wrong.

I've used benchmarking to help win over stakeholders and convince senior executives of a particular line of action several times. Making the most of benchmarking to educate stakeholders or win executive support isn't limited to quantitative data; qualitative data can be just as impactful in achieving your aims.

I could see the slight frown forming on Amandine's face as she tried to digest this last point.

"How do you mean?" she asked.

I decided to use an example from one of my previous seduction endeavours to expand on the point.

It was an event that ranked highly on my list of key learning experiences, one of the chief reasons being my discernment on the appropriateness of exploiting benchmarking information.

*

Some years after sorting out the PSN operations at Tempura Products, I was tasked with reviewing our worldwide logistics capabilities and requirements. At this time, Tempura had restructured its business model, adopting an integrated matrix structure spanning its entire activities globally. Yet there were cracks and leakages in a few areas – aspects of the business where alignment and cohesion were missing. Logistics was one of those.

I carried out the review with a fine-tooth comb. And it revealed a clear gap between our existing logistics capability and the requirements of our new business model. But I knew some powerful players had vested interests in keeping things as they were, because the status quo allowed them to wield undue influence. I didn't want my work to be a wasted effort; I had to convince the top brass to follow through and take action on the review findings.

When I presented my findings and proposal to members of our executive board, I included a qualitative benchmarking summary that showed our logistics capabilities and performance compared to our new business requirements, best-practice standards and our top competitors, covering strategy, governance and fitness for purpose.

This single slide starkly illustrated our gross inadequacies – we were laggards against our competitors by a wide margin, and our functional deficiencies were closer to worst practice, impeding our business strategically, operationally and commercially. It was a potent means of exposing our substantial shortcomings and the dire need to get our act together, a message the board just couldn't ignore.

Even as I write these words now, I still remember walking out of the boardroom with a smile in my heart.

The mandate I had secured was a terrific endorsement of the work I'd done with the help of several colleagues. And I looked forward to letting them know their efforts had borne fruit. Seeing the reactions of the executive board members, as I revealed far-reaching truths about our business that even they were unaware of, was also quite something. It had felt hugely rewarding to provide intelligence that they found illuminating. But the icing on the cake, the thing that really set my heart a-dancing, was the lavish praise from the Group Chief Operating Officer (COO). Amongst other things, he said he was "thoroughly impressed with the exceptional standard" of the work done and how "incisive" my presentation was.

I nearly had to rush to a hardware store to buy some strong chains to keep my ego in check!

I didn't though; I thought it'd be adequately curtailed by the cage of self-awareness and self-restraint I had been constructing for a while.

The COO's feedback was a glorious accolade. I sensed instinctively that recognition from a stakeholder like that would do my future in the company all manner of good. It was brilliant for my mojo.

Later that day, as I sat in traffic on my commute home, I was reliving the experience, smiling to myself in ecstasy, when my ego suddenly jumped out of its cage and attempted to get in the bath and take over the party.

It caught me unawares. But it was my own fault; I had been lost in my reverie.

Thankfully, being alone in the safety of my car, I was able to soothe it and coax it back into line.

My ego wanted to indulge in the customary chest-thumping everyone's ego enjoys – to a greater or lesser extent. But such vanity only fuels the ego's belief that we're the best thing since sliced bread, we're superior to others, or we're invincible, invulnerable, omniscient or omnicompetent. That's how we sometimes end up in ego clashes with some colleagues and stakeholders; because their egos, too, believe *they* are supremely and flawlessly superfly.

But none of us is really that superfly. Any of us can be brought down by a simple cold or a broken heart. And the simple algae and the humble bee both contribute more to life than any of us do.

My ego's predilection for vanity would only entrap me in a fallacy. Like the delusion of a mirage a lost traveller in the wilderness succumbs to. Vanity obscures wisdom, the kind of wisdom that is always inherent in our experiences of victory.

Naturally, it's pleasurable to wallow in the glory of our career victories. And there's nothing wrong in acknowledging one's accomplishments – it actually nurtures our self-belief, one of the key ingredients for career success. Appreciating your own talent and contribution at work will help you recognise the immeasurable capabilities within you.

That recognition was growing in me. But it was important to teach my ego to enjoy the victory party without spoiling it for my spirit and my long-term development.

So I cajoled my ego as you would a petulant child who isn't getting his way, just like I sometimes do with stakeholders.

I reminded my ego that the accomplishment would have been impossible without the contribution of others. We rarely, if ever, accomplish anything in life entirely on our own; other than breathing. We're all "carried", aided or supported in various ways – sometimes unseen or unexplainable – by others. Those others include a mysterious, unfathomable project team with inconceivable powers, made up of immortals like God, Allah, Big Bang, Brahman, Yahweh, Nature, Buddha, Gaia, Shàng Dì, Olodumare, Ik Onkar, Ahura Mazda and a few other team members. And the various ways we're aided include being given opportunities, guidance, encouragement, valuable talents, positive traits, auspicious circumstances, lucky chances, challenges and love.

Of course, we're also aided in many obvious and ordinary ways by more earthly mortals like our work colleagues and stakeholders.

Thinking that we're superfly to the extent of accomplishing our victories or work agendas *entirely of our own accord* is a dangerous habit that can contaminate our relationships with stakeholders; because it feeds "lone ranger" tendencies, and can inexorably and unnoticeably start to taint how we think about our stakeholders, how we feel about them and how we interact with them. It's like an unwelcome ingredient that changes the flavour of our stakeholder relationship dynamics. People tend to sense these vibes eventually, which can lead to an erosion of any goodwill and trust capital we've built up with them.

I also reminded my ego that, after satiating itself with self-glorification, it was more important for my growth and development to consolidate the learning the event had provided. And perhaps the salient lesson was that the experience reinforced my belief that, sometimes, one of the easiest ways of winning stakeholders over is simply to do an outstanding job.

Amandine clearly agreed with me on this. She nodded affirmatively, with a contemplative look on her face.

"Educating stakeholders with benchmarking information, like I did on that occasion, obviously helps secure alignment and buy-in," I continued. "At the same time, the positive changes in their perceptions mean that you're also influencing stakeholders' emotions."

Another critical lesson from that experience was my application of CRM principles. I remembered that when I was preparing my presentation to the executive board I had kept cautioning myself that the COO and other board members were my customers, because I was "supplying" them with information – albeit I wanted that information to yield a particular outcome. I repeatedly asked myself, "If I was in their place, what would I need to see and hear in the presentation that would move me to endorse that specific outcome?"

I made sure my presentation addressed this question robustly, in addition to portraying our logistics image from the perspective of our business customers.

# CHAPTER 16

It was experiences like my logistics task at Tempura that underpinned my staunch desire to ingrain customer-centric values as part of our functional DNA in my Global Operations organisation at Ostara Industries.

As we progressed with consolidating and optimising our global footprint, I kept pressing my regional managers to constantly ask themselves, "Where is the voice of our internal customer(s), and the external customer, in what we're doing and how we're doing it?" Our activities, processes and the attitudes and behaviours of our staff must make it easy for stakeholders to "do business with us".

The same values and principles apply to you and your dealings with your stakeholders, whether they're individuals or functional groups, just as they applied to Amandine and her stakeholder interactions.

It's the adoption and application of these principles that help make successful consumer brands flourish and prosper. They're really savvy at customer-centric CRM, because they know where their daily bread comes from.

They also want to keep the bread flowing and have it buttered on all sides. That's why they perpetuate a positive brand image with their stakeholders through effective public relations (PR).

And so should you.

Amandine's eyes lit up with interest when I mentioned PR as part of one's stakeholder management tactics. I reckoned something in her intuitively sensed the relevance. Perhaps because by then she had understood the importance of stakeholders' perceptions of one's personal brand in the workplace.

Whether we like it or not, we live in a world where perception can often be more important than reality. And it applies in most, if not all, facets of life; including our work lives and our romantic lives. The blossom of love that unfolds to enwrap the wooer and the wooed is often more strongly influenced or driven by their respective perceptions of each other than the reality of their characters. And we all know this, somewhere deep down inside of us. That's why we knowingly and unknowingly show our love interests the best sides of ourselves during courtship. It's the same impetus that leads organisations to tell us about the best aspects of a job and its benefits package when they're selling the role to us. And it's the same impetus that motivates those consumer brands to continually show their best sides and assure their lasting success by exploiting PR.

Perceptions matter.

They matter to the blossom and success of romantic love as much as they matter to the blossom and success of stakeholder love.

Yet positive or favourable perceptions don't happen by accident or luck, but by dedicated effort.

In the marketing world, effective PR is about influencing and managing perceptions, to build and sustain a favourable position in the target audience's feelings and opinions of a product, service or organisation. In the world of work, where you, your work agenda, your department or your project are the "product", "service" or "organisation", and your stakeholders are the target audience, this translates into reputation management – leveraging astute PR to position you and your agenda in stakeholders' consciousness such that their perceptions and sentiments about your groove are favourable.

Always remember that every touchpoint you have with your stakeholders can tarnish or burnish your brand. Because everything you do and say, and what your stakeholders think, feel and say about you or your agenda, impacts your brand reputation.

And remember, too, that your brand-building efforts must be backed up with meaningful outcomes, as I've indicated several times; for example, work results that are pertinent to stakeholders' worlds, will help address their problems, will resonate with them and can be substantiated. Otherwise you create dissonance between your brand promise and the reality, causing stakeholder dissatisfaction and damaging your brand reputation.

Selling a brand proposition that doesn't match the outcomes or results delivered is like touting a sports car to a customer only for him to discover it's been built with a scooter engine.

That's not astute PR, nor good reputation management.

Think about your PR game plan as a proactive and sustained undertaking to shape and protect your brand reputation with three principal goals: boosting awareness and understanding of your agenda amongst your stakeholders; influencing their opinions, inclinations, attitudes and, hence, behaviours; and maintaining goodwill and support for you and your agenda across your stakeholder base.

PR is vital for your work success because in today's organisational landscape it's often no longer adequate to be doing a good job; you must also be perceived as such. As John D. Rockefeller, the famous American tycoon, stressed, "Next to doing the right thing, the most important thing is to let people know you are doing the right thing."

\*

Letting people know you're doing the right thing or "taking care of business", delivering requisite, noteworthy or laudable outcomes, means you've got to showcase your contribution or blow your own trumpet, ensuring your stakeholders hear the harmonic notes of the melody you're producing loud and clear.

It's like concocting and executing a seamless combination of tuning into and understanding the corporate buzz or organisational dynamics; leveraging your understanding to win fans and cheerleaders in the right corners and echelons of the organisation; effectively communicating your work activities to stakeholders, with emphasis on the benefits to them and the wider organisation; and using ethical self-promotion to create success stories of your accomplishments and broadcast those stories widely such that the right ears hear of your triumphs.

Amandine's ears evidently heard my message, and it had penetrated her mind. She'd been listening thoughtfully, nodding every so often and occasionally making notes or asking me questions.

I knew she had been trying out many of my guidance points in her stakeholder interactions, with a noticeable degree of success. I'd been hearing positive comments about her and her work around the place.

She often bounced into my office to share her latest seduction victory with me, smiling from ear to ear as she recounted the details.

At times she sounded as if she herself couldn't quite believe the outcomes she was getting by imbibing these points into her stakeholder engagement style.

And as one would expect, sometimes things didn't go as desired. But there was a clear pattern of progress evolving in her stakeholder dealings.

I was particularly pleased that she was mingling with her stakeholders more. Yet she also appreciated that her efforts might not always change the relationship dynamics immediately, because attitudes don't change overnight.

She had recently hit a key milestone on her project, getting all-round agreement to pilot her newly developed Supplier Performance Management process with a couple of suppliers in one of our business units. She was thrilled at the prospect of constructing her first success story – she wanted to exploit the milestone attainment, seeing it as an opportunity with multiple benefits: it'd be good publicity for her project; it provided an avenue to advance the organisational readiness for the full-blown process implementation later on; and it'd help sway a handful of doubting Thomases in her stakeholder community.

I couldn't fault her thinking. She was on the right track. And it was another indication that she was growing in leaps and bounds.

Now she asked me for some concrete demonstrations of using PR effectively with stakeholders, to help her devise and polish her game plan.

In the course of time, I've come to learn that there are so many opportunities to ethically utilise astute PR to stimulate stakeholder love and help the love bloom. But we're often so much in a hurry that we miss many such golden prospects. We forget that quite often in life, to make swift progress we have to go slow and focus on the path.

When you go slow, you see more. And the more you see, the more you'll realise that your PR approaches should centre on disseminating a *structured flow* of information that always positions your work in a positive light.

Aside from informal avenues, like the casual conversations we have in the corridor, in the canteen or at the printer-photocopier, for example, some other possible PR vehicles to exploit include things like periodic update briefings with relevant senior players or the whole executive team; roadshows and other forms of publicity days with targeted stakeholder groups; features, news items and article stories on the corporate intranet website, the company magazine, the employee newsletter or other similar internal publications, or on the departmental or project intranet website; stakeholder testimonials and interviews in the same publications; a dedicated cyclical newsletter or regular e-mail updates; and publicity slots at appropriate corporate events.

I advised Amandine to think widely about other such openings she could capitalise on and not limit herself to the examples I had given. I told her that she would probably find it effective to use a mix of different channels as appropriate to the specific context – for example, she had to keep in mind factors like the nature of the message or portrayal she wanted to get across, the timing of her communications and the happenings and norms in the organisation.

Then I provoked another of her infectious chuckles and a shake of her head when I said the golden opportunities for PR leverage are like those golden moments we seize to display our best sides to love interests during courtship.

I elaborated that spotting such opportunities and taking advantage of them had been essential to me in reconstructing the PSN operations at Tempura Products. For example, as part of the revamp of our functional procedures, I introduced two new, critical, multi-departmental processes to strengthen our operational governance. They weren't just new to the PSN department, they were completely novel to Tempura.

I consulted my key stakeholder departments when I was developing the processes. So they were not only well aware of what was coming, but felt a sense of co-owner-ship because of their involvement. Yet when launching the new processes I still made sure they were both widely publicised, for example, on the corporate intranet and via a structured e-mail campaign.

One of the other publicity channels I used was a series of roadshows I ran across several sites, to spread the word amongst our wide community of stakeholder functions, like Engineering, Manufacturing, Marketing, Finance and Logistics. I made a point of focusing my presentation material and my own words on the benefits these new governance procedures would bring to each of these functions and the organisation as a whole. And at every roadshow event, I allowed plenty of time to take questions and address any concerns the folks had. After the main roadshow tour, I followed up with several small-er group forums where I walked some super-stakeholders through each of the new processes in greater depth.

That PR approach was the linchpin that assured the smooth and successful uptake of those two new governance mechanisms, right across several depart-ments – mechanisms which were highly instrumental in rounding up the erstwhile crazed cattle and bringing sanity to the Wild West chaos I had stepped into.

"I guess you can imagine what this did for the perceptions of our PSN transformation programme and my own personal brand," I concluded.

We got up to grab coffees, and Amandine checked her voicemail messages on her mobile phone as we walked to the coffee counter in the canteen.

There was a coffee machine nearby, but the stroll to the canteen was a nice break and a chance to stretch our legs.

On our way back, I started to tell her how I was weaving golden threads of positive PR into the fabric of the ongoing Global Operations optimisation at Ostara.

For example, I had got my IT Business Partner to implement a global functional intranet website, accessible in all our business locations worldwide. It served as a repository for information which my staff and stakeholders in all countries would find useful – things like our organisational structure; our policies, key processes and tools; our goals for the financial year and our performance scorecard; key contacts for specific, important issues or ongoing initiatives; and our activities on the optimisation programme.

Some of this stuff sounds mundane. Yet experience has taught me that one of the major sources of frustration – for both stakeholders and staff – is typically lack of clarity on simple things like who's responsible for what, who to speak to about "XYZ" issue or what's going on with some specific project or work initiative.

And it can be much worse when it's a global organisation, and worse still when the organisation is going through change.

The Global Operations website cascaded into functional and regional areas mirroring my organisational structure. So there were click-through sections or regional websites for our "Global Quality Management" functional team, for example, as for our "Americas" regional organisation. And wherever appropriate, each regional intranet site was either in the local language or included translated versions of the webpages, such as Spanish for our Chilean operations.

The intent was to shine a light through our organisation and activities. It was part of my endeavour to make it easy for stakeholders to do business with us, while providing a platform to publicise our wins. So, for instance, as we made progress with our worldwide optimisation, I made sure to broadcast key steps or attainments – usually through succinct announcements or news items on the corporate site that hyperlinked to more details on our functional website, always flavoured with golden specks of positive light that shone beautifully on us.

Amandine would gain a lot and sparkle like a diamond by basking under some of that light, and I told her so. It would serve her project well.

But I knew she was ahead of me and already thinking along similar lines. And I was keen to help her turn her ideas into reality.

I gave her an account of actualising my PR ideas while I was resolving the PSCM problems at Ribbexo Aerostructures. In that situation, activities like the town hall briefings and inviting some stakeholders to attend our Supply Chain team meetings undoubtedly helped our PR. I also developed and introduced a fortnightly *Supply Chain Update* e-newsletter as part of my PR game plan. It went out by blanket e-mail shots from the IT department, so all stakeholders right across Ribbexo could see what the Supply Chain team was up to.

Initially, it served as a vehicle to increase awareness of our intent and key actions with regard to tackling the chronic PSCM problems that were threatening the survival of the business. This information was extremely useful to appease many exasperated stakeholders – like chocolates and flowers, it helped to convince them of our commitment to bring sweetness and joy to their work lives.

Later on, when we had started to gain traction with addressing some of the root-cause issues, the newsletter became an excellent instrument to fly our flag, showing that there was substance behind our flowers and chocolates, not just an empty promise.

For example, when our on-time delivery to customers increased for three consecutive months, signifying a definite improvement trend which was also evident elsewhere, the achievement was a major feature story in the *Supply Chain Update* newsletter.

I used the opportunity to plug some words of praise from the CEO, who had given his positive feedback at my last update briefing to the executive team. Amongst other things, it indicated to the wider audience across Ribbexo that the top man himself was now a Supply Chain cheerleader.

I also included a few comments from some of the Supply Chain managers, along with their photos – it was their hard work, together with their teams', that had yielded the result.

But perhaps the sweetest of all sweetness for me was the testimonial from the Pharaoh himself, Greg Morgan. I used his words of endorsement for the Supply Chain team from his interview, and added in some nice comments of my own on how the cooperation and support from the Sales and Marketing folks had been a major contribution to our *collective* accomplishment.

"It was my way of making him and his team shine," I said to Amandine. "Because nothing fans the flame of stakeholder love like a boatload of appreciation, validation and recognition. It's simply another way of *giving* love, the greatest gift of all."

I could just hear the build-up of yet another chuckle on its way.

# FEEDING THE HUNGRY SPIRIT

# CHAPTER 17

IT'S AMAZING TO THINK THAT the Grand Poobah, the Almighty Pharaoh, a stakeholder who had been regarded as "the most difficult", ended up providing a glowing testimonial for the Supply Chain team at Ribbexo. And I didn't even have to build a temple in his honour, perform any rituals or offer any prayers or sacrifices to him, even though pharaohs are supposed to be divine, believed by many to be gods on earth.

I suppose we are all gods on earth in some ways, gods capable of outstanding accomplishments.

But the challenges we face – in life and at work – often make us forget who we truly are.

Typically, it's because we give so much more of our attention to "looking outside" than "looking inside". Our fixation with a challenge or its origins can have the insidious effect of reinforcing and amplifying the challenge, feeding it energy through our attention, and making it so gargantuan and dominant that we begin to doubt our ability to overcome it. Our doubt starts to chip away at our self-belief. And often, this is all happening below the surface.

It happens to all of us from time to time, not just when we're battling stakeholder challenges.

We must learn to trust ourselves steadfastly, undeterred by the doubts that may be niggling away at our minds – even when we've made "mistakes" or "wrong" decisions, or when we face a devil of a challenge and we're quaking in our boots. The growth of our wisdom is in experiencing the challenge or the apparent wrongness of our decision or action.

Just trust yourself.

If you don't trust yourself, how can you possibly expect your stakeholders to trust you?

And how can you expect others in general to trust you with the career opportunities that'll form your success and shape your destiny?

Lack of self-trust impairs the flourish of the human spirit. But no man-made challenge is bigger than the fire of your spirit.

As I've experienced and witnessed repeatedly, the very same challenges that make us forget who we truly are can also expose the awesome capabilities within each and every one of us; depending on how *we choose* to respond to the experience.

Thinking about my own experience with Pharaoh Greg Morgan reminds me how easy it can be to misjudge people and situations, or jump too quickly to conclusions which prove to be erroneous. It's an easy trap to fall into, an intrinsic pitfall of the multifaceted issue of stakeholder management and winning people over to one's work ideas, intents or plans. Greg is just one example from my experience. I suspect you've got similar examples of your own from your career experience.

Whatever the case, it's important for us to remember that stakeholder challenges may not always be what they seem initially. As my encounters with Greg Morgan and Ralph Patrick prove, these occurrences can sometimes yield bountiful and unexpected outcomes. And perhaps more importantly, stakeholder challenges almost always provide us with opportunities to learn and grow. But we've got to be able to see past the "wrapping paper". This often requires us to dig beneath the obvious and be open to new ways of seeing or perceiving life, especially our life at work.

My perception of work colleagues and stakeholders has undoubtedly expanded over the years. These days, when I think of taking people on a change journey I'm reminded of the African proverb: "If you want to go fast, go alone. If you want to go far, go together."

The archetypal mad scientist locked away in his laboratory may scoff at the wisdom of those words. Maybe he can afford to. But since few of us work in solitude like him, it's impossible to "go alone" in the workplace; whether we're going on a voyage of change or just dealing with the everyday tasks of our jobs.

Organisations are about people, first and foremost. And, as I've highlighted several times, our colleagues and stakeholders are exactly that: people. To be successful in the job and really enjoy our work life, we've got to be good with the "people" side of work – and, for most of us, more so than the "technical" side.

I remember explaining this in my book *Career Dreams to Career Success*. I likened the need to balance the people and technical aspects of work to what any successful car mechanic has to do.

Our expertise or knowledge of the technical aspects of our work is akin to the expertise the car mechanic has about, say, a spring compressor, transmission jack or voltmeter. It's a proficiency she has developed from her training and subsequent years on the job. But you wouldn't keep taking your car to that mechanic's garage if she had a lousy attitude or despicable behaviour. No customer would.

Her know-how with technical tools like the voltmeter and her mastery in diagnosing and fixing car problems make her a "mechanic". But to ensure her garage business remains successful over the long term, the mechanic must also be able to interact with her customers and manage their concerns and expectations with reasonable levels of consideration and decency, i.e., she must also be good with people no matter how great she is technically; otherwise she'd stunt the commercial success of her work.

The same applies to us all.

Professionals who are technically adept but lack good people skills hamper their workplace effectiveness. They typically have stunted careers. If you can't get people on board with your work agenda, then your technical knowledge is of limited value. Good people skills are like the favourable winds that sail your career ship, whatever the destination port you're aiming for.

Right from the early stages of my career, I set my sights on a destination that forced me to get to grips with people-related issues. I couldn't have known how stretching and painful some of the experiences would prove to be. But the pain was always the kind of "sweet pain" mountain climbers feel in their aching muscles as they progress upwards, ever closer to the magnificent view awaiting them at the mountaintop. The kind of sweet pain whose rhythm keeps you going because you know you must bear it to attain your career destiny. Just as the metal bears the blows of the blacksmith's hammer to become a valuable tool. Just as the land bears the dark night to see the glory of the next sunrise. Just as the tree bears the loss of its leaves to survive the cycle and thrive in the coming seasons.

I couldn't have thrived in my career without the sweet pain of those challenging experiences. Every ache of the pain was a window into wisdom; because every single challenge added something to my stakeholder management toolkit.

Having great mentors like Ralph also helped immensely. I'll be forever grateful to him for helping me learn to leverage interpersonal dynamics and detect hidden agendas when dealing with senior-level stakeholders.

Funnily enough, the stakeholder conflict which led to my remarkable mentoring relationship with him wasn't the first time life had thrown me a blessing disguised by its wrapping paper. I'd had a somewhat similar yet very different experience many years earlier.

If you've read my book *Procurement Mojo®*, you may remember me mentioning Harry Hughes. But I didn't share the details of the stakeholder challenges that were central to that experience. The hard knocks I got from those stakeholder battles were like stepping stones that led to Harry's door.

Harry was the Production Director of F&C Systems International, a small manufacturing business in South London in the UK. He'd been brought into the business to overhaul the company's operations. He had been driving a complete revamp of the outfit with great success, but he could see that the materials management aspects – basically, planning and managing the company's stock: from raw materials, through production batches on the shop floor, to finished goods – required dedicated focus. He recruited me specifically for that purpose.

For my part, I was excited at the chance to make real, tangible impacts on a business. It wasn't the sort of opportunity most graduates get straight out of university.

I had originally planned to secure a graduate job with a blue-chip company, where I would gain valuable learning on a structured graduate development programme. But the opportunity with Harry was too good to pass up. I had just spent my last few months at university setting up a computer simulation model of a Materials Requirements Planning (MRP) system as my final-year project. The job with Harry offered me the chance to do the same thing in real life – my core task was to implement an MRP computer system in the company, coupled with structured materials management disciplines. How sweet!

Or so I thought.

# CHAPTER 18

I STARTED MY JOB AT F&C Systems so full of enthusiasm. But my enthusiasm was soon punctured, as I struggled to win the staff over and convince them to adopt the new ways of working I was trying to introduce. University had taught me loads of stuff about materials management; I knew the theory inside out. But it hadn't taught me anything about winning friends and influencing people. And it was obvious from my inability to sell my agenda to the workforce. It wasn't long before I grew disenchanted and demoralised.

My feelings probably showed through in my frequent exhortations to stakeholders across the business. On several occasions I heard myself almost raising my voice to a production operator: "I've told you a thousand times, you must book the works order through the MRP system as soon as the job is finished!"

If it wasn't a shop-floor operator or supervisor, it'd be Isabella, the vivacious, young blonde in the Sales Office. She had a habit of sashaying down to the shop floor to alter the specified production items or quantities by scribbling on the printed works orders, with complete disregard for the MRP system.

Confronting Isabella always had the same outcome. She would beam me a coquettish smile and hold my gaze with an alluring look and a hint of devilishness in her doe eyes before making any effort to respond.

I always got lost in those eyes for a split second, with my senses transported to exotic realms by the bewitching notes of her perfume and the enchantment of that look. It was a captivating combination of elegance and an indescribable aura, a certain *je ne sais quoi* that made my imagination run amok amid incipient fantasies.

But I could see the trouble lurking behind that look. It was the kind of trouble carried and exuded by the pretty-but-naughty girls way back at school. The kind of trouble that reels you in like the flame lures the moth.

It was exactly the kind of trouble my sanity preferred to avoid at all costs. So, yet again, I'd reiterate to her the importance of using the MRP system properly and beat a hasty retreat before her beguiling charms got the better of me.

Walking away from Isabella always left me with a residual feeling of ambivalence, heightened by the lingering fragrance of her perfume in my nostrils. It was a scent that promised many things, so different from that of Tom McCarthy's cheap aftershave. I spent enough time with him to know. As the Purchasing Buyer, Tom was one of those stakeholders whose work tasks relied heavily on the MRP system, and impacted it to the same extent. I spent countless hours educating him on MRP principles and training him on using the computer system, all to no avail. I might as well have been engaging with a brick. Except bricks don't nod their heads and agree with you as if they understand what you're teaching them.

Whether or not Tom really understood remained a mystery to me for a long time. He persisted in ignoring the purchase requisitions generated by the MRP system. Instead, almost daily, he'd go to the materials stores to do a quick-and-dirty physical stock count, and then place purchase orders with suppliers based on his intelligent assessment of materials requirements.

"Tom, you shouldn't do that; you'll end up ordering too much stock or creating materials shortages if we don't all work to the MRP system!" I'd say to him almost every day. He'd mutter something incomprehensible and slink away to avoid a confrontation with me.

On other occasions, I'd discover materials deliveries from two or three days earlier still sitting unattended at the Goods-In department, which messed up the related stockholding and materials planning data on the MRP system. And yet again, Marcus, the Goods-In Clerk, would give me some cock-and-bull story about the Israelites crossing the Red Sea as his excuse for not booking the deliveries in on time. I was so incensed by his apparent irresponsibility that I sometimes found myself drawn into verbal wars with him. If my memory serves me correctly, I think he even went to see Harry on a couple of occasions to complain about me. This did nothing to endear him to me. If anything, it made me hate his guts even more.

These feelings of bitterness partly reflected my inability to separate the person from their behaviour or the problem at hand. My professional immaturity prevented me from appreciating that Marcus, as a person, was probably a decent chap, even if I found his seemingly recalcitrant work behaviour exasperating.

Perhaps if I had been more experienced and organisationally enlightened, I'd have been able to handle Marcus better using the subtle art of diplomacy practised by humanity for as long as man has traded wars and wares. But at the time, I was ignorant of the wisdom enshrined in the words of Italian diplomat Daniele Varè: "Diplomacy is the art of letting other people have your way."

If I'd been more professionally mature, unencumbered by the shackles of my ignorance, I could have used my little understanding of human nature to advance my agenda without inciting unwanted disputes and emotional aggro with Marcus. Same as with other stakeholders in the organisation whose actions contravened the work procedures I was introducing.

The more these non-compliances went on, the more it made my blood boil. And the ensuing conflicts, no matter how minor they were, increasingly left me feeling debilitated and extremely frustrated.

*

My feelings of frustration were partly directed at Harry himself. As my boss and the head honcho in the big chair, I couldn't understand why he didn't just instruct the staff to "Do as Sigi says".

Well, as I would come to learn from my future change management experiences, aligning stakeholders to a change agenda by coercion rarely works in the long term. It certainly never creates change that sticks.

As the big boss, Harry could indeed have used his big stick with the staff, and I could have ridden that wave to make them toe the line. But aside from the fact that bully-boy leadership is rarely effective, I myself would have missed out a great deal. I would have missed the opportunity of contending with organisational resistance and the rich pickings of learning the experience proffered.

I wouldn't have learned, for instance, that simply telling stakeholders what to do is never going to be as effective as touching them in their hearts and minds so they "get it", i.e., selling the agenda persuasively. This typically requires influencing people through emotional connection, in addition to hard data or facts.

Many of us often fail to appreciate and leverage the power of emotional connections when we're caught up in the demands of everyday life at work. It doesn't help that a lot of our conventional education and training tends to focus on the rational aspects of work – based on reasoning or logic. It becomes easy to be fooled into approaching all stakeholder issues from a purely rational or logical stance, using our reason or the thinking part of our brains. But there's another part of the human brain, an older part, called the "emotional brain" or limbic system, which plays a more significant role in our decisions and behaviours than many of us laypeople realise.

Yet those numerous professionals, thousands of university faculties and millions of specialists trying to get a handle on the human species have realised this.

Overwhelming evidence from neuroscientists, psychologists and sociologists confirms the irrefutable effect of emotions or feelings in modulating human relationships and exchanges. And, of course, it doesn't just apply to our families, friends and lovers in our private lives, but also to people we interact with in our work lives, as I've indicated several times.

Well before the experts of modern times, the ancient Greek philosopher Aristotle provided wise counsel on the important role of emotions in our interactions.

Our interactions with colleagues and stakeholders at work typically entail some form of persuasion, even when we're not doing it consciously in our engagements or communication. Persuasion is a fundamental element of interpersonal dynamics, one of the key forces at the heart of human interactions. And Aristotle's guidance from centuries back remains invaluable: "The fool tells me his reasons; the wise man persuades me with my own."

He explained that humans are inherently social animals, and we're regularly impelled or obligated to persuade other human beings or win them over for all sorts of reasons. He identified three distinct types of proof persuasive people use: *ethos*, *logos* and *pathos*.

*Ethos* is about your ethical dimensions as a participant in the dance of human interactions – your character, ethics and reputation, for example, are all crucial factors which impact your persuasiveness and ability to hit home with your stakeholders. Aristotle's assertion that "We believe good men more fully and more readily than others" has stood the test of scientific research. But it's a stakeholder's perception of you as "a good man or woman" that counts, not your perception of yourself.

No matter how virtuous, groovy or sexy you see yourself, if your stakeholder views you as a bad 'un, a jerk or as despicable as they come, you'll have an impossible time getting anywhere with them.

*Logos* relates to the substance of your communication – the actual words or language you use and the logic of your gist. This isn't just about hard facts, data and statistics; things like analogies, quotations, metaphors and stories are great examples of other ways of getting into your stakeholder's head persuasively to build concurrence. Yet it's the logic of your gist from your stakeholder's perspective that matters, not the way you see it.

You might think you're making sense with your story, but if your argument sounds like gibberish to your stakeholder's ears, then your chances of getting through to them are on a par with the chances of teaching a coyote to dance salsa.

*Pathos* pertains to the emotions you stir up in your stakeholder. Persuasion and alignment may come about when your communication strikes a chord and arouses their emotions. Fear, guilt, desire, anticipation, joy, inspiration, and so on, are all emotions everyone feels. Appealing to your stakeholder's emotions can be a particularly potent channel to get into their heart and touch them at their core.

Marketing maestros have known this for a long time. That's why the most memorable and successful media adverts are often those that appeal to our emotive sentiments.

The ability to blend all three modes of persuasion – *ethos*, *logos* and *pathos* – is a key aptitude for effective communication and savvy stakeholder management. Yet the heartstrings in particular are such powerful levers in the human psyche; emotions resonate with our spirit and tug at us in ways that data, logic or reasoning often don't, or just can't.

Emotions like hate, anger and fear incite us into conflicts or wars of all sorts, wars between individuals, collectives and whole nation states. Emotions like joy and jubilation rouse us to sing, whistle, dance with abandon, or to notice and bask in the beauty of the magic around us in each moment, a magic that is also nestled in the capabilities within us. Emotions like peace imbue us with calm and serenity, giving us the inner silence to hear the call of the dreams of our hearts, and to see our latent success with clarity, as it waits patiently for us to take a step towards it, so it too can respond by taking two steps towards us, because it wants to embrace us just as much as we want to grasp it. Emotions like hope and faith inspire us to take that step and embark on adventures in search of our career destinies, fuelling us with courage and confidence to conquer the doubts and challenges en route, as we advance triumphantly on the journey to the sweet embrace of our success. And emotions like love make us show our beautiful best and put poetry in our souls, and it's in amongst the verses and rhymes of the poems that we discover the right words to get through to stakeholders successfully.

Maybe that's why Aristotle stated that "A speaker who is attempting to move people to thought or action must concern himself with *pathos*."

The wise old Greek knew a thing or two about getting in the groove with the magnificent beings that people are – people like you, and your stakeholders.

Tapping into your stakeholders' emotions can often be far more compelling than relying solely or inordinately on bucketloads of data or logic, or counting on your job title or position, your good looks or your swagger. And if you have established a sound reputation – one of integrity, credibility, empathy, sincerity and trustworthiness – then you'll find it all the more easy to win stakeholders over.

Oh, how I wish I'd known all this stuff way back then at F&C Systems. Not just the smarts about heartstrings, keeping my personal brand groovy, and coyotes and salsa, but also the other lowdown, like the limited value of the big stick, the utility of diplomacy and the futility of verbal wars.

It sure as hell would have saved me a heck of a lot of aggravation and negative sentiments.

Yes, I wish I'd known …

But I didn't.

And because I didn't, my approach was worse than trying to teach the coyote to dance salsa; it was more like trying to teach it to play the ukulele. Hence the frustration and demoralisation that followed. Despite the energy and enthusiasm I had arrived with, and all the technical knowledge in my head.

The roar of the fire in my belly and my abundant passion for my work had inexorably compelled me to pour my soul into the job. And all I had to show for it was deep dissatisfaction and unhappiness, which dampened my flames to mere embers and took the wind out of my sails.

The experience crushed my spirit. Or so it felt, in the abyss of despondence I'd sunk into.

But the negative sentiments of my experience were the wrapping paper that yielded something else.

# CHAPTER 19

HARRY WAS AWARE OF MY drama all along. In fact, he later told me that he had deliberately let me loose to try things my own way, because sometimes that's how we learn best: from experience. He obviously knew about learning jungle survival by stepping into the jungle.

He decided to step in too and bolster my survival efforts when he felt my experience had given me enough hardship and he could see I was getting hopelessly demotivated. He started counselling me on effective change management, particularly winning stakeholders over and getting my results through people who don't report to me.

He taught me about taking the time and effort to walk a mile in stakeholders' shoes, especially when dealing with employees in the trenches. It's a fantastic conduit to really grasp their take on one's work agenda and what they truly think and feel about it – these are critical factors which are often overlooked or given scant attention yet have a major impact on the ease and success of any initiative that significantly affects people's work.

Even if your work doesn't entail introducing changes to your stakeholders' responsibilities or job activities, it's still absolutely crucial to appreciate others' perspectives at work – especially when you consider that someone in a different position or job role from you could likely have a different point of view from yours.

In some senses, an organisation with different departments is a bit like a house with different rooms. Two people standing in different positions in the same room are unlikely to have *exactly the same* views due to their differing vantage points. Those differing viewpoints get even more varied if the two people are standing in different rooms.

Sometimes we can be so resolutely locked into our own viewpoints or blinkered by our self-importance that we lose the ability to recognise that there just might be other views; our way may not always be the best way nor the only way.

It's an important issue that I've found myself highlighting many times with coaching and mentoring clients, employees in client organisations and delegates at my talks. And I've found that one of the simplest ways to illustrate the power of appreciating others' perspectives is with the simple business card. If I hold a normal business card up to you and ask you what you see, you will probably describe it as "a business card" and, maybe, read out what the card says – the name, job title, company, and so on. But I, on the other side of the card, will see something different: a blank card on the reverse side. Yet we'd both be looking at the same card. Of course, if we swap positions each of us will be able to see what the other had seen.

Keeping your mind open to the possibility of "other views" when dealing with your stakeholders will help you recognise that you may only ever be noticing or considering "one side of the business card", or one or two aspects of what is often a multifaceted work issue, task or situation.

The ability to acknowledge such possible alternative points of view that others may hold is one of the strands of emotional intelligence, a vital requirement for healthy intra- and inter-personal relationships. It's an extremely powerful mechanism that'll aid your personal effectiveness, particularly your ability to get a fix on your stakeholders first before pushing your own game plan. In essence, it's what Harry was trying to embed into my thick skull during our chats.

Sitting in his office listening to him back then, I could see the sense in some of what he was saying, especially when he used my everyday interactions with Marcus, Tom and my other stakeholders to exemplify his points, the same interactions that had started to corrode my soul. Little did I realise that over the ensuing years the stuff I was learning from him would lead me to many profound insights into the areas of personal effectiveness, winning people over and work success.

I know now that the big-stick approach must always be a last resort; and that if you understand your stakeholders' perspectives, drives and motivations, you'll be much more able to shape your agenda to address their fears and their needs, and hence make your work more meaningful and relevant to them.

I also know that building interpersonal chemistry with individual stakeholders always helps. Stop for a minute and think about one of your difficult stakeholders – what do you actually know about them as a person?

Building interpersonal chemistry means showing an interest in them and getting to know them a bit on a personal level – perhaps, how long they've been in their job, a little about their career history, a bit about their home lives, how many kids they have, their personal interests outside work, where they went on their last vacation, the name of their pet orangutan, and so on.

As long as your interest isn't driven by a desire for titbits of gossip, or your attention doesn't make you come across as a prying and intrusive busybody, you'll find that people in general appreciate others showing an interest in them or making an effort to know them. It's one of the verities of life, and somewhat part of being human. We all like to feel valued, treasured, acknowledged, esteemed or loved. We want to feel that we matter.

The need for attention and affection may be natural – we see it in so many places around us in nature. We see it in many animals where newborns instinctively seek out their mother's presence, whether for warmth, protection, nourishment, comfort or reassurance. We see it in human infants who get unsettled or agitated when they temporarily lose maternal contact, but become less distressed or even tranquil when their mother returns. We see it in children in the garden or playground when they yell in delight, "Dad, Dad, look at me! Look what I can do!" We see it in our own adult behaviours at dinner parties and other events, where we gravitate towards people we know, almost on autopilot, or we warm to new faces who show an interest in us by smiling, talking or listening to us.

We humans are born with brains that are biologically hardwired to respond to positive strokes like care, kindness, interest or the warm acknowledgement of others. It's in our groove. And we're more likely to hold positive sentiments of people who evoke the sweet vibes that such positive strokes typically bring. It's just the way we roll, part of the alchemy of life, recognisable in your own orientation towards those work colleagues and stakeholders who show you some love.

When you're *genuinely* solicitous about your individual stakeholders, or interested in their stories, and you make a little effort to get to know them, you're like an alchemist propagating the chemistry of positive interpersonal connections – connections propagated through the ages, helping to keep humanity sane; connections which in your own work context can only benefit you and your cause.

It can be time-consuming, and just isn't possible with every individual stakeholder in every situation. But it's an endeavour worth its weight in gold.

You'll be astonished how a bit of effort to create connections at an individual or personal level can spawn enormous improvements in engagement and alignment, because connecting with individual stakeholders on a personal level fosters affinity. It also enables you to tailor your engagement in order to create concurrence in individuals' consciousness, especially the content, language and packaging of your communication.

Even basic things like learning to say "Hello", "Thank you" or "Goodbye" in a foreign stakeholder's local language can make all the difference to the chemistry of your interactions.

But using clever packaging for your communication isn't just about what you say. As with your colleagues and stakeholders, your own non-verbal communication or body language – such as your facial expressions, posture, gesticulations, and so on – accounts for well over fifty percent of your communication. *How* you say it can be as important as, if not more important than, what you say.

When we speak, things like our tone of voice, our pace of speaking, the intonations in our speech and the volume of our voice convey more than we may be aware of, and may transmit what we don't intend to communicate – as may our overall body language. Yet it can be far worse or better when we don't speak at all.

Knowing when and how to speak and when and how to be silent is a key aspect of maintaining the right attitude when communicating with stakeholders.

Silence, at the right moments, even if just a brief pause, is a potent communication device that can sometimes achieve more than words. It also helps us listen better and retain more of what is being transmitted to us – whether the transmitter is a stakeholder at work, a loved one at home or the sage within us. So our chances of capturing and benefitting from every morsel of the communication to us increases significantly.

Looking back now, I'm so glad I was able to stay mostly silent and take in what Harry was transmitting to me all those years ago; even though I didn't fully recognise the virtues of silence.

# CHAPTER 20

SINCE THOSE INITIAL CHATS WITH Harry, experience has taught me that sometimes our conflicts with colleagues or stakeholders are simply rooted in divergence of views or differences in personality. And things can be made worse when we fail to appreciate the cultural nuances that come with stakeholders from other countries or cultures.

Cultural sensitivity helps. Tremendously.

It certainly helps when you're dealing with stakeholders from countries with a national inferiority or superiority complex. And if you're Anglo-Saxon, for instance, it helps too when dealing with stakeholders from some Mediterranean regions whose overly relaxed attitude to punctuality is similar to the "African time" that prevails in many parts of Africa and the Caribbean. If you're from certain parts of Asia, it helps when communicating with stakeholders from some erstwhile Eastern Bloc countries whose directness may seem awkward or rude. If you're Scandinavian, it helps when you have to engage with your more effusive or exuberant American stakeholders; and it'll help even more when you have to deal with stakeholders from tactile cultures – you may find yourself disliking their tendency for physical contact or their touchy-feely nature.

At the end of the day, it all comes down to one woman's meat being another woman's poison. What may be culturally appropriate in Jacksonville in the USA probably won't wash with a stakeholder from Johannesburg in South Africa, and you may find yourself struggling to have effective interactions unless you recognise and work with these nuances.

One of the ways to make use of some of these perceived differences is to mirror your stakeholder's body language when you're in conversation. For example, their gestures, posture or vocal pitch. Mirroring is another good mechanism to help build rapport and attune someone you're interacting with, as several studies have shown.

But it's got to be subtle to be effective; you shouldn't try to mimic someone's gestures exactly, for instance, or try to mirror their precise posture or every single iota of their mannerisms. That would be trying too hard, which will distract you from paying close attention to their gist.

It's always imperative to not allow the gist to be clouded by the seeming peculiarities of your stakeholders.

In any case, whatever those peculiarities are, cultural or otherwise, it's amazing what you can learn from people who seem quite different from you or embody a contrasting or incompatible value system.

And none of the perceived differences are "bad", "wrong" or "right" anyway. Many of those differences often contain wisdom, magic and miracles. Just look at successful love relationships and close friendships you know of that epitomise the phrase "opposites attract". And then look at the many symbiotic relationships in life between organisms that are so "different", like the bee and the flower: neither the bee nor the flower worries that the other is different or peculiar, they just get on with their groove – the flower feeds the bee with pollen and nectar, and the bee helps the flower to reproduce and prosper by spreading its pollen.

The parties in these mutually beneficial relationships signify the wisdom of life, a beautiful wisdom that is available to us all – if we're tolerant, unprejudiced and humble enough to countenance the notion that, just like us, and just like the bee, and the flower, our stakeholders have a birthright to be who they are. We're not better, more important or more intelligent than the bee, the flower or any one of our stakeholders. They each have their own unique intelligence and contribute something to life. And we do not control the menu of life; the menu was designed by inexplicable forces beyond the realms of the human mind.

Alas, the human mind often thinks it is our lord and master and it knows it all. And because the mind has our best interests at heart, it is constantly probing, assessing, plotting and scheming; for example, on ways to handle our stakeholders. Yet our minds *cannot* understand everything that happens in life, especially the affairs of magic and miracles. There are some issues in the alchemy of life that exceed the logical capacities of your rational mind, things which your second brain which resides in your gut can often sense.

It's unfortunate that too many of us have become prisoners of our minds, trapped by our logic or rational reasoning. And when we do realise we're in captivity, trying to escape can seem like riding a wild bronco. Yet many, too, have escaped the prison.

Those who escape tend to be those who realise that the constant scheming and chattering of the mind is another source of "noise" or interference that buffets and bamboozles us ceaselessly, impeding our ability to tap into the wisdom of the sage within us.

Yet whenever we're able to fade out the noise, even if only momentarily, we harness perhaps the greatest virtue of silence: perceiving the gigantic river of knowledge in us with clarity, a river from which we can drink infinitely to leverage a knowledge beyond reason. Each sip of the drink helps expose our best self and expands our capabilities, including our ability to propagate stakeholder love. That's why escapees escape.

Perhaps you're one of the escapees.

Or maybe you're hatching your escape plan right now, and your inner guru has led you to these pages to aid your efforts.

As you continue to grow and expand your perception, unfettered by the chains of your reason, you'll find that it's wiser to seek out the magic in those differences or peculiarities of your stakeholders because some things just symbolise the very fabric of life. Acorns grow into oak trees, not banana trees. Butterflies evolve from caterpillars, not earthworms. Human babies develop into adult people, not adult grasshoppers. And people feed their hearts with dreams, fulfilment and love, not hate. These things, these wonderful little miracles of life, and many other such phenomena, are things we can't fight or resist, things which are just the way they are, things which often add sugar and spice and everything interesting to the flavour of life. Especially the things to do with people.

Rather than driving yourself insane with the forlorn hope that a stakeholder will change and become who, what or how you think they should be, it's more effective to focus your energies on learning to accept them as they are, even if you don't quite understand them, and nourishing the relationship. After all, none of us are perfect, not even those of us blessed with voodoo magic powers – we still have to bear the blessings and burdens of being human.

As fellow human beings, we share many similarities with our stakeholders. And we often lump them together as "stakeholders" in our deliberations, as if they form a completely homogeneous group. Yet each individual is unique. So, personal, cultural or dispositional differences will always exist. Building interpersonal chemistry or growing the rapport with individual stakeholders is a great way to counter those differences. It can also provide insights into the "scripts" playing out in individuals' hearts and minds, and how comparable their scripts are to ours.

Our scripts are the *subliminal* programming of our worldviews – our beliefs, values and how we perceive and interpret life, including our work life – which we pick up unknowingly from the environments we've grown up in, biologically and professionally. For example, that stakeholder who grew up in Jo'burg may now be living and working in Jacksonville; her worldview – and consequently, her attitudes and behaviours at work – are quite likely to be strongly influenced by the script of her cultural and societal upbringing in South Africa. She'll need to be conscious of this and make whatever adjustments she deems necessary if she is to thrive in her professional career in the USA.

In the same way, some managers who spend their formative professional years in organisations where autocratic leadership prevails end up embodying similar regressive, bully-boy leadership styles when they themselves become senior leaders. It's the old "monkey see, monkey do" syndrome. These professionals unknowingly develop a flawed script of what effective leadership means, and end up carrying this imprint throughout their careers; unless they are subsequently exposed to other, more progressive environmental influences and make concerted efforts to rewrite their scripts.

Similarly, many people who spend a significant part of their early careers in small businesses or entrepreneurial cultures, where structure and formality tend to be minimal, or ramping up growth through creativity necessitates a fluid modus operandi, often find the discipline of structured organisational procedures quite stifling when they move to larger, mature businesses later in their careers. The script they've picked up from their years in a distinctly different organisational climate could make them prone to maverick behaviours or non-compliant work styles that may lead to all sorts of difficulties – difficulties which could become "stakeholder challenges" for their work colleagues like me and you.

Our scripts are highly potent forces that shape our personal bias, predispositions and perspectives. Quite often, in our interactions with work colleagues and stakeholders, we sow the wrong seeds or read the signs wrongly simply because we may be handicapped by the ramifications of our own scripts. Additionally, many of us rarely ever remember, beforehand, that each one of these interactions is a fertile opportunity to create a delightful experience and bathe the relationship in the perfume of positive vibes. And afterwards, we seldom ask ourselves what fragrance we left behind.

Becoming aware of how your past and present environments and related scripts subliminally influence your thinking, inclinations, perspectives and actions is a powerful aid to your self-leadership.

And getting some insight into individual stakeholders' scripts helps you "sprinkle gold dust" at every touchpoint – whether it's an informal chat at the coffee machine or an experience of doing business with you – rather than cultivating all sorts of negative emotions that typically characterise stakeholder conflicts, the same sorts of emotions I suffered in my early dealings with Tom, Isabella and other stakeholders at F&C.

It took me many more years after my time at F&C to fully understand all these factors and how they affect my work success.

But that understanding grew from the initial counsel I got from Harry.

\*

I didn't appreciate at the time that Harry was mentoring me, nor the long-term value of the wisdom he was imparting. I just felt happier with the guidance he was giving me.

What I learned from him helped me turn that job at F&C Systems from what had felt like an occupational and emotional fiasco into the first major triumph of my career. The MRP implementation that had been fraught with various setbacks – usually related to people ignoring or abusing the computer system – got back on the rails and was fully completed. Shortages of production materials diminished to almost nothing. And stock accuracy improved unrecognisably, so much so that I sometimes found myself doubting and triple-checking the results of the periodic stock-check programme I had implemented.

My doubts were unfounded though. If I didn't believe the stock-accuracy figures and the other performance measurements, I could easily have looked to my stakeholders' behaviours as alternative indicators of the improvement. Tom, for example, seemed to successfully wean himself off his daily "quick-and-dirty physical stock count" habit, something he had been doing since birds learned to fly. It was as remarkable and gratifying as a junkie coming off drugs. The Finance Director stopped looking at me funny; he no longer had opportunity to, as the previously routine summons to his office to explain sizeable stock losses and write-offs petered out. Marcus and the production guys visited my desk every so often, typically to flag up discrepancies in supplier deliveries or inaccurate item part numbers, or to seek my guidance on something else; more often they'd collar me on the shop floor for the same reasons or to tell me their latest dirty joke.

There were many other similar changes in attitudes and behaviours with stakeholders across the company. People had started to trust the MRP system, and more importantly, adhere to it.

But their trust grew because the system was reliable. Yet it "became" reliable because they started to adhere to it and participate in maintaining its integrity – increasingly so, as a direct result of *my own change of approach*: I had given up the idea that a coyote could play the ukulele and had been putting Harry's advice into practice instead.

The more I "practised", the more fantastic my results seemed, which grew my confidence and inspired me to practise even more.

I felt like a cool cat. Whereas I used to look up to the gods above asking why they let me suffer, now I looked up smiling in gratitude – the kind of deep thankfulness you feel when you wake up from a nightmare and realise it was only a dream.

Indeed, my coyote-training days seemed like a bad dream in retrospect. Life as a cool cat was so much sweeter. Unimaginably so.

Experiencing that transition was like drinking the sweet nectar of victory in a land of smoke and ashes. My spirit threw off the dark shroud of dejection that had previously curtailed its flourish. And the embers of the fire in my belly roared back to life. I felt my heart grow wings and soar with the angels, as it danced the dance of joy and fulfilment, celebrating the success that my learning had yielded. And I continue to leverage and build on that learning to this day.

Harry and I became good friends and enjoyed a wonderful mentoring relationship for many years afterwards – exactly the same thing that happened with Ralph later on in my career. And in both cases, life gave me a fabulous mentor who emerged from stakeholder conflict situations.

As painful as those situations were at the time, I'm grateful for what evolved from the experiences; not just the mentors I ended up getting, but the learning I gleaned – learning that served me well in subsequent jobs and contributed immensely to my career development and fulfilment, learning that you're now harvesting as you read these words, words that will hopefully touch your spirit in all the right places.

Immeasurable capabilities abound in the human spirit, the same spirit that brought us the steam engine, penicillin and the internet, the same spirit embodied in all the great souls of renowned accomplishments through the history of time. That same spirit resides in you.

You, me, your husband, your wife, your child, your lover, your mum, your dad, your best friend … every one of us is filled with the hungry spirit of human potential that thirsts for fulfilment. A big part of fulfilment and success at work is a better sense of self and more harmonious, collaborative relationships with our colleagues and stakeholders.

When we reflect on our work and career adventures, it's worth remembering what we've learned from our stakeholder engagements and how those experiences have helped to feed our hungry spirit and nurture our continued growth.

What have you learned?

As I sit here writing these words, I know that one of the most important things I've learned is that my success at work has never been solely dependent on my technical knowledge or competence; my ability to manage stakeholders effectively has *always* been an essential part of the mix. And I've heard the same thing from countless professionals at the top of their game in various spheres of life.

I've learned also that life is created in each moment. When we interact with colleagues and stakeholders at work, we're creating moments that will become memories – the memories that'll form a big part of our life story. It's good for our work life if those moments are productive, and it's even better for our spirit if the memories are pleasant ones, and better still if they're memories of sweet stakeholder love.

Each moment is like one of those footprints in the sand, and we choose where the footprints lead. The magic charm or special spark of our mojo is a destination that constantly beckons.

Always remember to steer your footprints towards your fulfilment and your best self, the one that stakeholders will want to love. And in the heart of each moment, right as you place your foot in the sand, remember, too,

that your long-term career growth will be strongly determined by your proficiency in managing your stakeholder
relationships. You'll go a long way by mastering the tips
and tactics in this book, all the way to the sweet embrace
of the success that awaits you.

# EPILOGUE

I HOPE YOU'VE FOUND THE anecdotes in this book valuable and informative. As a writer, I confess that a huge part of me would love you to have *enjoyed* these war stories too.

But quite honestly, more important than that, I feel a sense of obligation to pass on my insights in ways that will help you boost your mojo and sing the song inside you – the song waiting to be sung, by you and only you.

That was the motivation to share my knowledge as a story.

I learned a while back that knowledge doesn't have to be complex and heavy; stories help lighten the load of learning, often leaving indelible imprints on our consciousness and touching us in ways that subliminally guide our actions. It's one of the reasons many of us learned our earliest lessons about life from fables and children's stories like *The Tortoise and the Hare* or *The Adventures of Pinocchio*.

The adventures in this particular story weren't about me though. I don't claim to be an expert on stakeholder management. But I've had tonnes of experiences of stakeholder love – some sweet, some not so sweet – in transforming my life from an impoverished immigrant to a supposed demigod in blue-chip multinational companies. I think I learned a thing or two along the way. And those who've tried out my guidance seem to agree.

My fervent hope is that you will become one of them.

In sharing that guidance here, I've used the terms "emotions" and "feelings" interchangeably for the sake of simplicity, to let the gist flow nice and easy. And I've mostly done the same with "logic", "reason", "reasoning" and "rational reasoning", as with "logical" and "rational". I'm sure the purists will forgive me.

In any case, my use of artistic licence as such doesn't detract from the value and effectiveness of the lessons in the story.

I've mentioned some of these insights and tactics elsewhere, such as in my talks, articles, social media posts and media interviews. If you've read or heard my work before and any of the tips here sounded familiar, stop for a minute and think back to how you mastered spelling or multiplication at elementary school: chiefly by repetition. So going over these tips again here can only be good for your learning.

I definitely find it useful to keep reminding myself of these points, particularly when working on client assignments and dealing with a range of stakeholders, including those who stretch one's patience or tolerance like Greg Morgan and John Reed.

Your stakeholders are no different in general. They have the same two eyes and ears, one mouth, same behavioural tendencies, present the same challenges and have the same impacts on hitting your sweet spot at work.

If your stakeholder relationships are proving detrimental to your progress and success at work, the onus is on you to change the status quo. When you take responsibility for the status of your work life, you create a positive psychological shift – shifting from being a victim of the situation to becoming a shaper of the world you desire. Talk to anyone who has triumphed over great challenges to create lasting success in any realm of life and you'll hear the same message: making an effort to take control of the situation greatly amplifies your chances of creating the outcomes you want.

If after reading this far you still have any doubts about the efficacy of the guidance in this book, I invite you to do one thing: try it. Try incorporating the tips and tactics conveyed here in your work life and see for yourself what outcomes you get. After all, they do say experience is the best teacher.

Remember, just as you mastered spelling and multi-plication at school by repetition *and practice*, mastering the guidance in this book and sharpening your ability to nurture productive stakeholder relationships will only come from experience, i.e., by taking action and putting it into practice; otherwise the "learning" is not really learning.

If it seems difficult, remember that it'll only ever be as difficult as riding a bicycle was when you were learning to ride one.

You can imbibe what you've learned here into your future experiences with your stakeholders and harness the favourable winds that will sail your career ship on an auspicious course. You'll rewrite the story of your work life. And I have every confidence that it'll be a story of sublime success and fulfilment. Don't let anyone stop you – not even yourself.

I wish you an avalanche of victories and blessings on your career adventure; may the best days of your past be the worst days of your future.

\*\*\*\*\*\*

"When spider webs unite, they can tie up a lion."
– African Proverb

\*\*\*\*\*\*

# NOTES

THANK YOU SO MUCH FOR spending some of your most valuable assets – your time, your attention and your money – on this book. My intention was to create an educative and entertaining experience worthy of that investment.

If you enjoyed the book and found it useful, please share that with your colleagues, peers and friends. Also, I hope you can spare a minute to let others outside your circle know of your experience by posting a positive review on your bookseller's website or other relevant forums or social media platforms – I'd really appreciate that. Thank you.

\*

This is a work of creative non-fiction, drawing on my true experiences. The characters, events and circumstances are composites of very real occurrences and my creative juices. I have changed the names, details and determining characteristics of people, places and organisations to avoid hurting anyone and to maintain anonymity. And I have adapted some elements for literary effect while retaining the truthful essence of the actual experiences.

\*

I've tried to avoid using much technical lingo to keep things simple and sweet. However, I recognise that not every reader will be familiar with the few terms and acronyms I've used. So, here are my very simplified clarifications (if necessary, you can get more detailed explanations from reliable technical sources):

- ENTERPRISE RESOURCE PLANNING (ERP): An IT system or software package that organisations use to integrate, plan and manage most of their day-to-day activities, such as sales, purchasing, accounting, manufacturing, payroll, stock control, etc.

- MATERIALS REQUIREMENTS PLANNING (MRP): The granddaddy of ERP; an older and simpler IT system which focuses on fewer day-to-day business activities – MRP typically covers only sales, stock control, purchasing, aspects of manufacturing and finance.

- PURCHASE REQUISITION: A document created by an MRP or ERP system that tells the procurement/purchasing/materials management department what item to purchase from suppliers, the quantity required and the date the item is required by.

- PURCHASE ORDER: A document created from an MRP or ERP system and issued to a supplier, detailing the items the buyer wishes to purchase, the agreed price for each item, the quantity of each item required and the agreed dates the items should be delivered.

- SALES ORDER: A document created on an MRP or ERP system detailing the items a customer wishes to purchase, the agreed price for each item, the quantity of each item required and the agreed dates the items should be delivered.

- TOTAL QUALITY MANAGEMENT (TQM): A management approach or organisational ethos where a commitment to continuously improve quality is shared by every individual and baked into the culture, as a means of delivering customer satisfaction and long-term success.

- Works order: A document created from an MRP or ERP system that tells the production/manufacturing department what item to manufacture, the quantity required and the date the item is required by.

*

In addition to my first-hand experiences, I have also indirectly drawn on many sources – books, articles, mentoring conversations, research studies, etc. – which have influenced my thinking and approach over the years, or inspired me to develop and expand my perspectives. It's impossible to list them all, but I must mention the following, which have had a more direct bearing on my work in this book:

1. Aaker, Jennifer, "Harnessing the Power of Stories", *www.youtube.com*, Stanford Graduate School of Business, 13 March 2013.

2. Abinanti, Lawson, "Positioning Depends on Repetition and Consistency", *www.messagesthatmatter.com*, 10 January 2016.

3.  "Allan Luks' Helper's High: The Healing Power of Helping Others", *www.allanluks.com/helpers_high*, accessed 6 October 2019.

4.  Borg, James, *Persuasion: The Art of Influencing People*, Third Edition, Prentice Hall, 2010.

5.  Benedictus, Leo, "Look at Me: Why Attention-Seeking Is the Defining Need of Our Times", *www.theguardian.com*, 5 February 2018.

6.  Carter, Sherrie Bourg, "Helper's High: The Benefits (and Risks) of Altruism", *www.psychologytoday.com*, 4 September 2014.

7.  Carnegie, Dale, *How to Win Friends and Influence People*, Cedar, 1991.

8.  Cialdini, Robert B., *Influence: The Psychology of Persuasion*, HarperCollins, 2009.

9.  Coelho, Paulo, *The Alchemist*, HarperCollins, 2006.

10. Coleman, Nicole, "'Sadvertising' Pulls On Consumers' Heartstrings – And Purse Strings", *www.forbes.com*, 28 April 2015.

11. Conger, Jay A., *Winning 'Em Over: A New Model for Managing in the Age of Persuasion*, Simon & Schuster, 1998.

12. Corter Consulting, "Chief Indecision Officer" organisational chart [Illustration], as displayed via hyperlink in MacAskill, Andrew (@MacAskillful), "Great org chart covering #leadership during transformation lnkd.in/e4Z6CDr" [Tweet], *https://twitter.com/MacAskillful*, 11 December 2015.

13. Covey, Stephen R., *The 7 Habits of Highly Effective People,* Simon & Schuster, 2004.

14. "Do Ads That Tug at Our Heartstrings Really Make Us Buy More?", *www.adma.com.au*, 17 July 2017.

15. Enders, Giulia, *Gut: The Inside Story of Our Body's Most Under-rated Organ*, Scribe Publications, 2017.

16. Frahm, Jen, "5 Pitfalls of Change Communication to Be Careful of and One Huge Opportunity!", *www.cropleycomms.com*, accessed 19 January 2020.

17. Frankl, Viktor E., *Man's Search for Meaning*, Ebury Publishing, 2004.

18. Friedersdorf, Conor, "The Highest Form of Disagreement", *www.theatlantic.com*, 26 June 2017.

19. Gilbert, Paul, *The Compassionate Mind*, Constable, 2009. (Also, cited Bowlby, John, 1969, 1973, 1980).

20. Goleman, Daniel, *Emotional Intelligence*, Bloomsbury, 1996.

21. Grzyb, Jo Ellen, "Mail Shots", British Airways *Business Life*, Cedar Communications, March 2018.

22. Hammerstein, Oscar, II. "Happy Talk", *South Pacific* [Film]. Directed by Joshua Logan, South Pacific Enterprises, 1958.

23. Handy, Charles, *The Hungry Spirit*, Arrow Books, 1998.

24. "Helper's High: Why Doing Good Makes Us Feel Good", Project Helping, *www.projecthelping.org*, accessed 6 October 2019.

25. "How to Be Diplomatic", The Book of Life, *www. theschooloflife.com*, accessed 6 October 2019.

26. Ifould, Rosie, "Acting on Impulse", *www. theguardian.com*, 7 March 2009.

27. *Inside the Foreign Office*, BBC Two HD, 15 November 2018 (Daniele Varè quote by Sir Simon McDonald, citation on *www.twitter.com/ SMcDonaldFCO*, 29 November 2018).

28. Integration Training, *www.integrationtraining. co.uk*, "Real Organization Chart" [Illustration], as displayed in Perera, Mark (@markperera), "What's Wrong With Your Organizational Structure?" [Tweet], *https://twitter.com/markperera*, 6 June 2015.

29. James, Geoffrey, "How to Win Arguments Without Making Enemies", *www.inc.com*, 6 July 2017.

30. James, Oliver, *They F*** You Up: How to Survive Family Life*, Bloomsbury, 2003.

31. Kelsey-Sugg, Anna and Pryor, Cathy, "What Keating, Hawke and Clinton Can Teach You About the Art of Negotiation", *www.abc.net.au*, 21 August 2019.

32. Kambouris, Angela, "Trust is difficult to establish [...]" [LinkedIn post], *https://www. linkedin.com/posts/leadershipconsultant_trust-leadership-emotionalintelligence-activity-6633463504261263361-z90U*, accessed 13 February 2020.

33. Kotter, John, "The Heart of Change", *www.youtube. com*, 23 March 2011.

34. Krogerus, Mikael and Tschäppeler, Roman, *The Communication Book: 44 Ideas for Better Conversations Every Day*, Penguin, 2018.

35. Luft, Joseph, *Group Processes: An Introduction to Group Dynamics*, Third Edition, Mayfield Publishing Company, 1984.

36. Maurer, Robert J., "Why We All Just Need a Little Attention", *www.psychologytoday.com*, 18 November 2016.

37. McCann, Susan (@Susanjmccann), "We rebuke those who lie to us […]" [Tweet], *https://twitter.com/Susanjmccann*, 5 February 2020.

38. Moseley, Corey, "Everything You Need to Know About Workplace Friendships", *https://blog.jostle.me/blog*, accessed 21 November 2019.

39. Mullins, Laurie J., *Management and Organisational Behaviour*, Fourth Edition, Pitman Publishing, 1996. (Also, cited Alderfer, C. P., 1972; Janis, Irving L., 1972, 1982; Maslow, A. H., 1943, 1987; Warr, P., 1983).

40. Osagie, Sigi, "Boost Your Mojo, But Find It First! Strategies for Managing Your Growth and Development", motivational speeches at various CIPS branches, UK, 2010–2011.

41. Osagie, Sigi, *Career Dreams to Career Success*, EPG Solutions Limited, 2018.

42. Osagie, Sigi, *Procurement Mojo®: Strengthening the Function and Raising Its Profile*, Management Books 2000, 2014.

43. Osagie, Sigi, "Organisational Effectiveness and Capability", business talk for Hilton Worldwide International Supply Management Conference, Barcelona, Spain, 18 October 2011.

44. Osagie, Sigi, various articles, feature contributions and social media posts, previously published on LinkedIn, Twitter, Facebook, *www.sigiosagie.com*, *www.epgsolutions.co.uk* and several other media outlets, 2006–2021.

45. Rath, Tom and Harter, Jim, "Your Friends and Your Social Well-Being", *www.gallup.com*, 19 August 2010.

46. "Repetition and Consistency", *https://theageofideas. com*, accessed 11 January 2020.

47. Riegel, Deborah Grayson, "Want to Increase Your Presence? Start by Telling One of These Stories", *www.inc.com*, 18 December 2017.

48. Robbins, Anthony, *Unlimited Power: The New Science of Personal Achievement*, Pocket Books, 2001.

49. Schawbel, Dan, "Why Work Friendships Are Critical for Long-Term Happiness", *www.cnbc.com*, 13 November 2018.

50. Shellenbarger, Sue, "Use Mirroring to Connect with Others", *www.wsj.com*, 20 September 2016.

51. Strocchi, Giovanni, "Why Pulling on the Heartstrings Is Vital to Campaign Success", *www.mediatel.co.uk*, 7 November 2016.

52. "The Importance of Workplace Friendships", *www.biospace.com*, 16 February 2019.

53. Thompson, Jeff, "Mimicry and Mirroring Can Be Good or Bad", *www.psychologytoday.com*, 9 September 2012.

54. Vasel, Kathryn, "The Argument Against Having Close Friends at Work", *www.cnn.com*, accessed 21 November 2019.

55. Walton, Alice G., "Why Work Relationships Affect Our Mental and Physical Health", *www.forbes.com*, 13 October 2016.

56. Zak, Paul, J., "Why Your Brain Loves Good Storytelling", *www.hbr.org*, 28 October 2014.

# ACKNOWLEDGEMENTS

THERE'S AN OLD SWAHILI ADAGE that says, *"Asiyefunzwa na mamaye, hufunzwa na ulimwengu"*, which means, if a child doesn't learn the ways of the world from its parents at home, it will be forcibly taught the same lessons by the realities and hard knocks of the world.

I like to think that I'm fortunate to have learned from my parents as well as the Faculty of Hard Knocks at the University of Life. So I'm grateful to my parents and all the university teachers life has provided me.

Those teachers include lots of people who have helped and supported me through the years in various ways. That encompasses all the stakeholders I've worked with in my career, and I thank them all – both those who readily helped make my efforts successful, and the "difficult" ones who stretched me; by stretching me they helped me grow and expand my abilities. (If you're one of the latter group and you think you recognise yourself in this story, whatever the perceived portrayal my intent wasn't to offend or to make anyone look bad. Besides, this story is "faction" so it can't be you, can it?)

I'd also like to thank the mentors and wise ones I've learned from on my life journey, and express my gratitude to all my readers, clients and attendees at my talks over the years – the questions they've asked me and the feedback they've given after trying out my advice have been invaluable.

Special thanks to Craig Thomson, Darren Brackwell and David Abbott, who read my early manuscript and provided useful critiques that helped me refine my work.

And big kisses and voodoo love to the blessed angels in my fabulous publishing team, who transmuted the final manuscript into the book you're reading now: Karen "Elohor" Morton, an impeccable editor and a joy to work with; Tanja "Alafia" Prokop, a very wise woman and designer extraordinaire, who also believes in magic; and Graciela Aničić, an exemplary professional and an angel with a sweet voice – may your paths be filled with sublime happiness.

Finally, I give boundless thanks to Love, in all her manifestations; including the Gypsy Witch Earth Mother. She knows why.

# ABOUT THE AUTHOR

Sigi Osagie helps organisations and individuals boost their workplace effectiveness to achieve their business and career goals.

He has extensive leadership experience across several sectors and continents, including implementing varied organisational change and transformation projects. He previously held senior executive and board roles with a variety of blue-chip corporations and SMEs. His ground-breaking research on Management Effectiveness and Organisational Performance for his MBA informs much of his work.

Sigi arrived in the UK as a near barefoot and penniless immigrant; just fourteen years later he was a global director in a FTSE 250 multinational.

Today, he draws on insights from his atypical life journey and career success to inform and inspire others, through his work as a writer, speaker, business adviser and coach + mentor.

For more information or to get in touch with Sigi, please visit www.sigiosagie.com.

# Also by Sigi Osagie

***Career Dreams to Career Success: Conversations with a Mentor***

"★★★★★ Another inspirational read from Sigi! Full of useful tips"

— Amazon Customer


***Procurement Mojo®: Strengthening the Function and Raising Its Profile***

"One of the best procurement books of the past 20 years"

— Spend Matters Network


***25 Quotes & 75 Questions to Boost Your Thinking on Procurement Success***

"A great read and very practical!"

— David M., Category Manager, New Jersey, USA


Available at: SigiOsagie.com

Printed in Great Britain
by Amazon